# GRANDAD'S
# FRONT PORCH

# GRANDAD'S FRONT PORCH

## A MEMOIR OF BLOSE HOLLOW

William R. King

Printed in the United States of America.

ISBN 13: 978-1-59571-105-2
ISBN 10: 1-59571-105-8
Library of Congress Control Number:  2005938230

Word Association Publishers
205 5th Avenue
Tarentum, PA 15084
www.wordassociation.com

To have spent some time in Blose Hollow as a boy during the Great Depression was to have been privileged. Nobody told us we were poor.

**William R. King**

# ACKNOWLEDGMENTS

I am indebted to the following for adding so much to my stories and photographs about life in Blose Hollow, my sister, Carol Ann Smith, brothers Tom and Fred, and cousins Carolyn Blose, Tom Blose, Izorra Johnson, Betty Mumau, Marie Rorabaugh and Evelyn Vasbinder. A special thanks to Zarah Blair for the pencil drawing of the front porch, and to my wife, Judy, for her critque, proof reading and patience.

# CONTENTS

# INTRODUCTION

Blose Hollow is a real place, yet my story is more about a place of the heart than of geography. It's about ordinary people putting down family roots in a small, out-of-the-way valley in Montgomery Township, Indiana County, Pennsylvania. On a present-day county map it is where Blose and Wilgus roads meet.

Grandad's front porch was real, too, but no longer exists. My Uncle Revere, a long-time bachelor and school teacher who inherited the homestead, decided he would try married life in his retirement years. Shortly after his marriage, the porch disappeared. What a disappointment. The porch Grandad built extended across the entire front of the house. It was replaced by a tiny little thing with hardly enough room for two or three people. Gone was the place where I met so many new and different people, where

I first heard Grandad play the violin, bones and trumpet, where I marveled at how Ted Koozer could do so many things with only one arm, where I saw a human eye looking up at me from the porch deck which turned out to be Henry Gromley's glass eye, where I heard about feats of strength in the coal mine, woods and on the farm, and where I heard about Mrs. Farster running though the corn field holding her dress as high as she could so the corn would grow tall that year. Everyone at the porch was part of the community, and had his story to tell. There aren't enough front porches in America where friends congregate and grandchildren can get an education.

Marie Blose Rorabaugh grew up here, and shared many memories — especially about Blose School, which she attended and where her father taught. Marie enlisted in the Navy during World War II, later went to college and then taught school before getting married and raising a family. When I asked Marie what this place meant to her, she replied: "There was always a feeling of peace in the valley, a sense of belonging and serenity no other place could match." I'm sure my mother would have answered that question much the same way.

Most call this place "Blose Hollow," while a few prefer "Blose Valley." My mother would have accepted the word "hollow," as long as it didn't become "holler." That she would not abide.

The life we know in the 21st century is far different from the one my ancestors knew when they settled Blose Hollow in the 19th century. Simply getting from one day to the next was a struggle. Most everything they needed came from the land on which they lived. They had no luxuries. An early American saying that ruled their lives went like this: "Use it up, wear it out, make it do, or do without."

When the coal mine opened at Wilgus, it provided some cash income that helped greatly. But something that influenced their lives more than money was a one-room school built below the original homestead. It was given the name "Blose School," and a son and two grandchildren of Michael Jr. and Susanna Blose taught school there. We would call the building primitive by our standards, yet it broadened their horizons more than we will ever know.

One of the great disappointments in my mother's life was that none of her children settled in Blose Hollow.

Life and careers simply pulled us in other directions. In spite of that, it is the nearest place to home that I know.

# THE MOVE TO BLOSE HOLLOW

Sometime after the Civil War, my great-grandfather, Michael Blose Jr., and his wife, Susanna, gathered their six children along with what meager possessions they had and moved from Blanket Hill in Kittanning Township, Armstrong County, Pa., to nearby Montgomery Township in Indiana County. On today's roads, that would be a distance of about 50 miles. Some years later, their son Frank told my mother the trip took two days in a covered wagon with him and his brother Walter driving the livestock. Other than that fragment of information, there is little else we know about the journey.

Blanket Hill gets its name from real blankets left by frontier soldiers during the French and Indian War, when Col. John Armstrong destroyed the Delaware Indian village at Kittanning. On the march there, they sighted a band of indians at a campfire a few miles east of the village. Armstrong left a contingent of soldiers to watch the indians. While he and his men destroyed the village of Kittanning, the indians routed the contingent of soldiers, who fled and left their blankets at the campsite. The blankets were discovered later and the place has a state historical marker designating it as " Blanket Hill."

There is a story handed down in our family that Michael's older brother, Daniel, owned a large tract of timber in Indiana County, and encouraged Michael to come over and buy part of his timberland. Family stories have a way of growing. Exact size was never mentioned. Daniel's tract of land got bigger and bigger until, family legend has it, he sold it all and moved to California.

When I stopped at the Indiana County Courthouse one day, a very accommodating lady helped me find the various ledgers needed to learn about the land transaction between Daniel and Michael. We found that on Sept. 20, 1853, 148 acres of land in Montgomery Township was deeded to Daniel Blose, living in Kittanning Township, Armstrong County. The price was $470.

Then on April 2, 1887 – 25 years later – 148 acres of land in Montgomery Township was deeded to Susanna Blose, of Kittanning Township by Daniel Blose and his wife, Martha. The price was $1,200. They, too, were living in Kittanning Township. I confirmed this information with David Suckling, an attorney in Kittanning.

As far as Daniel going to California, for all we know he may not have gotten any further west than the Allegheny River running north and south through Armstrong County. More than once in the U.S. Census records, I found a Daniel Blose listed as a farmer living in Armstrong County. There is a soft marble tombstone for Daniel and Martha in the Christ Lutheran Church Cemetery in Kittanning Township. The numbers and figures are wearing away, but it is plain to see that Daniel lived to the ripe old age of 95, while Martha was 71 when she passed away.

Both Michael and Daniel did their part in making our country a melting pot of nationalities. Daniel's wife, Martha Sinclair, emigrated from Ireland, while Michael's wife, Susanna Wahl, came from German Prussia. Martha was one of the thousands of Scots-Irish who came to America in the 1800s. Susanna's homeland was a German monarchy. At the end of World War II, the Allied victors declared an end to monarchies in Germany.

Why did Michael and Susanna move to Indiana County? Why was it that just Susanna's name was on the deed? I asked attorney David Suckling about this, and with a devilish grin and a chuckle he said, "That raises all sorts of possibilities."

The place they left in Armstrong and the one they came to in Indiana are very similar in topography and soil. It seems they simply traded one set of stony hills and valleys for another. I think it was more personal than that. We will never know the answer to many of our questions because of fires. In those days, there were no building codes: overheated coal-fired stoves and flues caused much devastation. When a home burned, more than a place to live was lost, families lost valuable records, cherished keepsakes, pictures and letters impossible to replace.

Twice my grandparents' homes were destroyed by fire. Seeing two homes burned to the ground and then rebuilding from the ashes surely took resolve, fortitude and hard work. Grandad cut the timber for both those homes. Little wonder he was just muscle, bone and sinew.

We know Susanna was born in German Prussia, and came to America as a teenager. How she met and married Michael Blose Jr. is unknown. She was his second wife, and they had six children. She was Roman Catholic, small of stature and spoke broken English. Susanna died in 1891, four days before her 56th birthday. The story is told that when she lay dying, she asked her son Harry to go for a priest. Before Harry returned with the priest to administer last rites, his mother passed away. When they arrived, the priest refused to enter the home. That left a wound that took more than a generation to heal.

I regret we have no pictures or letters that tell us more about Susanna Wahl Blose. Something tells me she was a person worth knowing.

The family of Michael Blose Jr. and Susanna Wahl Blose:
    Michael Blose Jr., May 4, 1822 – Sept. 15, 1910
    Susanna Wahl Blose, June 13, 1835 – June 9, 1891
    *Their children:*
    George Francis "Frank," Sept. 3, 1863 – Oct. 11, 1943

Walter Michael, April 26, 1866 – Jan 23. 1934

James Henry "Harry," Oct. 27, 1868 – Feb. 25, 1961

Amelia Lousia, August 1870 – Oct. 6, 1893

John Lee, Aug. 1, 1872 – Oct. 25, 1962

Sarah Anna "Sadie" Oct. 30, 1877 – July 1943

I met all but Amelia, and am proud of everyone. There wasn't a slouch in the bunch. Amelia, also known as "Millie," married a man by the name of Jim Biss in 1892, and they moved to Wyoming. Sadly, her family back in Blose Hollow received a letter literally edged in black from Jim Biss stating that "poor Millie died at 12:15 p.m., October 6, 1893." She died of a uterine infection shortly after giving birth to a son. They named the son Carl, and sadly he died shortly after his birth. Millie's brother, Harry, went to Wyoming and accompanied the bodies back home. Harry never married, and Millie, Carl and Harry are buried side by side in Rowley Cemetery.

Uncle Frank moved a few miles away to a farm near Hooverhurst. He was married twice. He and his first wife, Amanda Walker (1865-1905), were married Nov. 1, 1884, and had seven children: Charles (1885-1887), Eva Blose Madill (1887-1973), Walter (1889-1950), Dollie Blose Rowley (1891-1972) Edith Blose Wright

(1893-1976), Daisy Blose Swank Tyger Ebert (1895-1978) and Irvin (1909-1903).

Uncle Frank and his second wife, Magdaline Buchanan (1878-1943), were married March 21, 1909, and had three children: Ethel Blose Catherman (1910) Mary Blose Hapner Lazotte Stiver (1913-2004) and Alden Dean (1916-1980).

At the time this is being written, Ethel Catherman, living in Erie, Pa., is the oldest living descendant of Michael and Susanna Blose. Uncle Frank and Magdaline both died in 1943, yet he is buried beside his first wife in Rowley Cemetery. Magdaline is buried in Montgomery Cemetery beside her first husband, Joseph Buchanan, who died at age 29. I'm told it was a common practice in those days to be buried beside your first spouse.

Uncle Walter married Mary Alice Bennett (1873-1958) on Dec. 21, 1895, and they had 12 children: Ralph Bennett (1896-died the same day), Murray Russell (1897-1930), James Newton (1899-1987), Lucy Blose Spicher (1901-1976), Walter Glenn (1903-1922), Everett Jerome (1907-1908), Mildred Blose Burns (1909-1984), Foster Eugene (1912-1999), Susannah June Blose

Gromley (1911- ), Mary Alice (1914-1919), Evelyn "Betty" Blose Mumau (1917- ) and Sarah Marie Blose Rorabaugh (1919- ). Three of their children, June, Betty and Marie are still living. After Mildred's husband died, she returned to live in the old homestead. Mildred had no children. It was a great loss to all when she perished in a fire that destroyed the homestead in 1984. Marie said two trunks filled with memories from both sides of the family were lost when the house burned.

Uncle Walter's wife outlived him by 24 years. We knew this kind and gentle lady as "Aunt Molly." My mother and her daughters were always close friends.

Murray enlisted in the Army during World War I, hoping to go overseas as a medic. Instead, he became a victim of the influenza epidemic that raged across the world in 1918. He was honorably discharged one year after enlisting, and never fully recovered from the illness – it seemed to plague him for the remainder of his life. For every American killed in World War I, 10 people died from the influenza and pneumonia that often came with it. The epidemic reached its peak in the last week of October 1918, when 21,000 people died. By the spring of 1919, the rampage of this deadly disease had slowed considerably. The deadly flu virus of 1918 has never been identified.

Among the scarce memorabilia I have are two copies of Murray's obituary and a 12-page letter he wrote to Uncle Harry in 1922 from Johnstown, Pa. Murray's penmanship was excellent, and the letter revealed a keen interest in politics. According to the obituary, 1,000 people attended the funeral service and 1,500 were at the cemetery. That is a remarkable number of people to have gathered on the hilltop where Rowley Cemetery is located. Obviously, Murray Blose had a wide circle of friends. The obituary was written in a manner not common to our time. Written in 1930, the following sentence expressed that manner and feeling: "When the bugle call was given, our friend who had often responded to that call, lay silent in his last resting place, for he had heard the call from above and his spirit had gone on to join the throngs that had gone on before."

Uncle Walter and Aunt Molly had two children who served their country in two different wars. Marie, their youngest child, was born in 1919 on her brother Murray's 22nd birthday. Marie enlisted in the U.S. Navy during World War II. I don't imagine that happened in many American families. Like many of us, Marie attended college under the World War II GI Bill, and she became a school teacher. Today, she lives near Burnside, where her sons have one of the largest lumber operations in Pennsylvania. Her husband, Bob Rorabaugh, passed away several years ago.

James Newton left Pennsylvania as a young man and settled in Oklahoma. As a boy I remember when he and his wife, Hazel, came back for the Blose Reunion. What I remember best was that man from the West with his cowboy hat. Their son, Mike, living in Stillwater, Okla., has done a masterful job of organizing the Blose family tree.

John Lee Blose, my grandfather, married Amanda Pearl Shaffer (1871-1940) on the first day of a new century – 1901. They had five children: Richard Lee (1901-1992), my mother  Sarah Lucretia Blose King (1903-1996), William Monroe (1905-1971), Paul Revere (1906-1997) and Adolph (1908-1909). This family, and the family I grew up in, mirrored each other. Both had four boys and a girl. The youngest in each family was a boy, and both boys died at about 2 years of age. My brother Jimmy died of pneumonia before antibiotics were available. People of my grandfather's generation were somewhat fatalistic about life. Once, when talking about one of our children, Grandad remarked: "He will grow up to be a fine young man – if he lives." Grandad had a reason for making this statement. I was surprised to learn the life expectancy rate grew by almost 30 years from 1900 to 2000. In 1900, the average lifespan was 47.3 years, compared to 77 in the year 2000.

Aunt Sadie married John C. Irwin (1871-1943) in December 1896. They had one daughter and two sons. Josephine, their daughter, was the only one to marry. She married William Roodhouse in 1923. He had the terrible misfortune of being gassed by the German's in World War I. That gas poisoning claimed his life while a relatively young man. Bill Roodhouse died at the Veterans Hospital in Aspinwall, leaving Josephine with two young boys, James and Robert.

Aunt Sadie and Uncle John's two sons were Harry (1900-1965) and John (1903-1982). I write about John and Harry in a separate story.

Michael and Susanna Blose had 31 grandchildren. Four, all women, are still living. The tide has turned. Women are now outliving men. As mentioned previously, Susanna died four days before her 56th birthday. Twenty-seven of her grandchildren were born after she died. By contrast, all my mother's grandchildren were at least young adults when she died.

# JOHN LEE BLOSE

It was a long time ago, and I was just a boy, yet I can still see him coming up the road. It is late afternoon; the road is dusty and so is he. His step is heavy; I am sure he is bone tired after a day of plowing on a stony hillside. Bringing his team, Dick and Prince, back to the barn, his first stop is the pump and the watering tub at the old wooden school house.

The man is my Grandad, John Lee Blose: farmer, coal miner, woodsman, musician, philosopher and storyteller. Although, on occasion he took a little too much whiskey, he was still loved by his grandchildren.

Once, when I was a boy, I trailed along to that stony hillside where he was turning the earth with a single-bottom, handheld plow. He made it look easy, so I asked if I could try my hand at plowing. Grandad gave me the reins and I grabbed the plow handles and took off. In less than six feet, a rock sent the plow out of the furrow. I simply lacked the strength, determination, and know-how to keep the plow in that stony soil. I gained new respect for him that day. He could keep going hour after hour while I only lasted six feet.

Grandad was not a big man. What there was of him was mostly muscle, bone and sinew, He carried no extra flesh; his exercise program was working the land, cutting timber and swinging a coal pick.

Outdoor work took so much of this man's day, it amazed me that he had the time to develop his musical gifts, He played three instruments: the violin, the trumpet and the bones. I expect few people have heard the bones being played. Sometimes they are made from real bone, but usually a hard, durable wood. Grandad used a set of four bones with two between the fingers on each hand and moved them to produce musical rhythms much like playing of spoons. His hands moved with great speed, and there were times when I thought I heard the bones talk.

On a summer evening, the front porch his auditorium, he would sit in a straight-backed chair and entertain whomever happened to be there with tunes like "Golden Slipper," "The Devil's Dream," and "Soldier's Joy." Nobody knows of Grandad ever having a music lesson. I often wonder what he would have become had he lived in another time and place.

Grandad was full of stories and had a sense of humor some may have thought a bit irreverent at times. It was up to the listener to separate fact from fiction. One of his many stories was a bit of verse about the creation. I made a few minor changes to make it politically correct for today's world.

It went like this:

"I came from old Virginny and I never went to priest school or any other college, but I can tell you one thing that is a moral fact: This world was made in the twinkling of a crack. He made the earth in six days, then, he made the sky, hung it overhead and left it there to dry. Then he made the stars out of a pretty wench's eye to give a little light when the moon didn't rise. Now lightning is a flighty gal – she lives up among the clouds, and thunder he's a reckless boy for he can holler loud. Now when he kisses lightning she dodges off in wonder, then he jumps and tears his trousers and that's what makes the thunder. Now the wind began to blow and the rain began to fall and the water got so deep it drown the people all. It rained for 40 days and nights exactly by the count and landed Noah's Ark on the Allegheny Mountain."

# AMANDA PEARL
# SHAFFER BLOSE

People who knew Grandma called her Pearl. She is not as clear in my memory as Grandad. He lived 22 years longer than Grandma, and when I went to the farm I spent little time indoors. I thank my cousin Ikey and older brother, Tom, for refreshing my memory.

Grandma's parents were William and Isabelle Shaffer, who lived near Hillside and later moved to a farm close to Creekside. She had three sisters, Elizabeth, Frances and Hutoca; and two brothers, Afton and Wallace.

I found it interesting as well as frustrating how the spelling of names changed from one record to another. In Beer's History of Indiana County, written in 1880, he spelled Grandma's name Sheffar and her mother was Isabella, not Isabelle. On the land deed, my great-grandmother's name is spelled Susanna, while on her tombstone it is Susannah. I asked a long-time geneologist about this and she said "Go with Susanna: She didn't have anything to do with the spelling on the tombstone."

Grandma was a short, heavy person, and obviously some of her descendants, including myself, picked up that trait. She had to have been a hard worker, because every meal was made from scratch. Grandma lived before refrigerators, indoor plumbing, electricity, supermarkets, frozen food and everything instant. She drew water with a hand pump and cooked on a coal stove that sometimes belched out clouds of black smoke. And from that infernal stove she produced some of the best homemade bread and pies one could ever eat. Her buckwheat cakes topped with "hog honey" were the best. If anything needed to be mixed, it was done by hand. It was an age of manual labor.

My cousin, Carolyn Blose, once remarked to Uncle Revere that both her grandmothers had to toil long and hard every day. Uncle Revere became rather indignant and replied: "I'll have you know, my mother never wanted for a thing." It depends on one's perspective.

Milking cows was a chore that often fell to Grandma. Of course, it was done by hand, and was done outside in nice weather. The cow I remember especially was Daisy. She had the coloring and ruggedness of a Brown Swiss. Daisy also had a big udder and large teats that were forever getting scratched and cut by briars. After milking, Grandma would give Daisy's wounded teats a liberal application of Porter's Pain King salve that was equally good for man or beast. The milking took place under a white oak tree. It still stands and gets more majestic with each passing year. A white oak growing in the open is a different tree from one in the forest. It develops huge, spreading limbs and makes a wonderful shade tree.

With few exceptions, everything Grandma put on the table came from the farm. This included wild huckleberries, blackberries, venison, rabbit, squirrel and even groundhog. On occasion, Grandad would come up with dried, very salty fish that came in a yellow wooden bucket. It had to be soaked at least overnight before Grandma would fry it. It was a different piece of fish from what you would get in a restaurant today.

Grandma stopped in the afternoon for a short nap. This would be on the front porch if the weather was nice. The noon meal was called dinner and the evening meal, supper. After supper, the front porch was owned by the men, women were welcome, but it was unusual if they tarried long.

In those days there was still a sharp distinction between the roles of men and women in American life. Men were providers, working mostly outside the home. Women stayed at home, except for certain farm chores and teaching school. Those breaking this pattern were the exception. World War II was the event that caused a shift in the roles of men and women in American life. Women started moving into the workplace, doing things normally reserved for men. That change has never stopped. I expect that many who lived in Blose Hollow before World War II would have found that change unsettling.

# THE BLOSE SCHOOL

The Blose School was just a stone's throw from my grandparents' back door. I expect it was given the name "Blose School" because it was built on their land. By today's standards, the building would be considered totally inadequate. There was a time when these little buildings were proudly referred to as "temples of knowledge." Without a doubt, this little school played a very important part in the lives of all those who lived in Blose Hollow.

The driving force behind public education in Pennsylvania was Thaddeus Stevens, who served in the U.S. Congress during the Civil War. Because of his leadership, thousands of schools like the Blose School were built across the state in the 1800s. They weren't perfect, but they filled an educational void in the lives of people living in rural Pennsylvania. Back then, that meant almost the entire state, except for the areas around Pittsburgh and Philadelphia.

I talked with many teachers and students who were part of the one-room school system. They gained my respect for they were truly pioneers in public education. Those who taught were not only teachers, he or she was the principal, the guidance counselor, school nurse, music teacher, head custodian, athletic director and in charge of anything else that needed to be done. They certainly were not burdened down with bureaucracy. For the most part, they were on their own with no vacation time or sick days. My mother taught at the Brickell School in Montgomery Township. During the 1922-23 school term, she had 77 students and was paid $85 a month.

Like most schools, the Blose School had eight grades in one room. There were usually around 30 students. However, the Blose and Brickell schools were exceptions because they were located near Upper and Lower Wilgus, both active coal-mining towns. Miners, immigrating mostly from Eastern Europe and Italy, had children who increased this number to almost 80 at times. What an educational melting pot and challenge that must have been. Whether it was 25 or

80 students, there was still only one teacher. They succeeded because there was a sense of community, cooperation and tolerance.

Upper Wilgus was one of those once-thriving western Pennsylvania coal towns that have literally disappeared from the face of the earth. My mother said when she was growing up, it had a post office, a skating rink, a Grange Hall, a hotel, a store owned by the coal company, an Italian store, a third general store, a meat market, a millinery shop, a barber shop and a ball field. How amazing that all these places have disappeared. Nature has taken back Upper Wilgus, and her children are scattered across America. Chickasaw, a very similar town in neighboring Armstrong County, has suffered the same fate.

Among those I interviewed were my cousins, Betty Blose Mumau and Marie Blose Rorabaugh. Both attended the Blose School for eight years. One of their memories was "The Letting." Uncle Walter Blose, their father and Grandad's brother, taught at several schools in Montgomery Township. Each spring, the family looked forward with great anticipation to "the letting". This was a meeting of the school directors when they decided where each teacher would be teaching in the township. Teachers did not stay in one place. I expect they were moved around more than they wanted.

Recently, I read where a university teacher said a child entering a one-room school with an incompetent teacher would be stuck with that teacher for eight years. The statement is simply wrong and misleading.

Agnes Galbreath had a long teaching career starting at age 18 in Boggsville. I talked with Agnes at length, and one of her statements was "The school board moved us around." She had many positive things to say about teaching in one-room schools, and said her time in one-room schools were "The most rewarding years of my life."

I expect there were a number of reasons why teachers were moved. Discipline was one. Uncle Monroe, Grandad's son, told about a teacher at Blose School who was unable to maintain order. The school directors replaced that person with a man by the name of Marshall Hamilton. On his first day at school, he gave the students free rein. It was bedlam. When school was over, Hamilton said "This was your day, the rest are mine." Discipline returned to Blose School.

Hamilton later owned a soft-drink plant in Gypsy and a beef cattle farm elsewhere in Montgomery Township.

In addition to my great-grandmother, I would like to have known Marshall Hamilton. As with Susanna Blose, something tells me he was a person who made a difference.

There were many in the history of the valley I would like to have known, but I'll add one more to my special list: Uncle Walter Blose, Grandad's brother. He died in 1934 because of injuries suffered falling off a load of hay. My recollection of him is all too faint. Uncle Walter was the first of many school teachers among the descendants of Michael and Susanna Blose. He was also a foreman in the coal mines, farmer, and leader in his church. He must have been a person of high character. I would like to have been on the sidelines listening to Uncle Walter and his three brothers discussing the important issues of the day.

Apparently there was a period of time when the school directors in Montgomery Township frowned on female teachers getting married. Recently I talked with Erma Spicher Gearhart, an alert, petite 103-year-old. She was graduated from Indiana Normal School, taught one year in Montgomery Township, got married and lost her teaching position. She said the directors told her they could not have married female teachers. They could do things then that would never be allowed today.

When the public school movement began, there were no colleges where future teachers received an education. Teachers were hired at the discretion of school directors. When the position of county school superintendent was established, that person hired the teachers. There were some good teachers, but still too many lacked the learning and skills needed to teach. Eventually academies were established where those who wanted to teach received instruction. Now progress was being made. Purchase Line in nearby Green Township had an academy. After the academy came two-year normal schools. My mother and many others in this part of Pennsylvania attended Indiana Normal School. Later it became Indiana State Teachers College, and now Indiana University of Pennsylvania.

Indiana State Teachers College, the successor to the Indiana Normal School, played a part in my life as well as my mother's. After World War II, I enrolled at

Penn State under the G.I. Bill. They were short of room at Penn State, so I was farmed out to Indiana for my freshman year. That year, 1947, there were 1,415 students at Indiana. That included 941 veterans and 474 regular students. I was one of nine Penn State freshmen. It's doubtful we will ever know the full impact the World War II G.I. Bill had on America. It started right off in the college classroom when some professors didn't quite know how to handle veterans who were mature and ready to learn on the first day of class. Many of us ignored the ritual of freshman initiation.

There were more students attending Indiana Normal School in 1915 than when I enrolled there many years later. According to Stephenson in his History of Indiana County, more than 1,500 students were enrolled in 1915, and a 1916 Normal School advertisement said $200 covers all expenses for one year, excepting books, for those preparing to teach. Others pay $260. The Normal School graduates were going out to the hundreds of one-room schools across the commonwealth.

A typical day started with a Bible reading, after the ringing of the school bell. After the Bible reading, there was the Lord's Prayer, the Pledge of Allegiance and then singing, usually "America the Beautiful." There might be more singing, depending on the teacher.

Great emphasis was placed on student recitation. I'm sure this was a time when younger students listened and learned from their older classmates. Marie Rorabaugh said she could recite the entire Gettysburg Address in fourth grade. I'm sure when she did this other student were listening very carefully.

Like every school, Blose School was not without its moments of humor. Once a teacher was having trouble getting an arithmetic problem through to George Colgan, so she decided to take a different approach. "She said, 'If you reached in your left pocket and found a nickel, then reached in your right pocket and found a second nickel, what would you have?'" George replied, "Somebody else's pants."

Visitors were not uncommon. Once, Luther Heberling, son of my mother's half-sister, came visiting with a bantam rooster. There was an inner vestibule with a knot hole, and Luther put the rooster's head through the knothole into the school room. Neither Luther nor the rooster could get the head out, and it started to crow. Needless to say, all learning stopped. Being a visitor was the only thing that saved Luther from the paddle.

Someone said there were four subjects: reading, writing, arithmetic and "stick." This has been oversimplified. There were other subjects such as geography, history, spelling and music, depending somewhat on the teacher. There was only so much one person could do. And yes, the teacher was allowed to discipline with the paddle or "stick."

The bell that once called the students to school now sits on a special pedestal below the old schoolhouse. The property is owned by Mark Stebbins, a great-grandson of Walter Blose. The bell is special because there is a piece broken out as seen in the photograph. This happened when the Armistice was signed at the end of World War I. The bell was rung so long and so enthusiastically that a piece fell out. Imagine what a celebration that must have been. I wonder how they got the word? With automobiles being a rare thing, and no telephone, I'll guess somebody carried the message down the road on horseback from Hillsdale.

Comparing the rural one-room school with today's consolidated school is like comparing a Model-T Ford and a new Lincoln Continental. Both will get us to our destination, but what a difference in time, convenience and comfort! Yet I expect the Model-T was appreciated more in its day than the Lincoln is in our day.

Indoor plumbing was one of the many luxuries not found in the Blose School. The restroom was the celebrated privy located outside in back of the school. That never was a place to tarry in either hot or cold weather. The drinking fountain was usually a hand pump located near the school entrance. An effort in health education was to have students bring their own drinking cups. Still a common cup was often used.

Words like cafeteria, auditorium and gymnasium were not part of the vocabulary. Lunch was carried from home. Hopefully, there would be a field nearby where students could play baseball, one of their favorite activities.

Electricity would not arrive until about 1940. If light was needed, oil lamps would have to do.

The teacher and students got to school as best they could. There were no "snow days." Travel was usually on foot, sometimes in a buggy or on a horse over dirt roads and dirt paths.

A big, pot-belly coal stove heated the school. Boys were always glad to go outside for a bucket of coal. The coal used was soft bituminous coal probably from the nearby Wilgus mine. The coal fire could easily smoke up a room if the draft and flue weren't regulated correctly. In spite of your best effort, there were times when a coal stove would defy you and smoke up the room. Was keeping clean a problem with the coal stove and messy floors after teaching in snow and mud? Marie Rorabaugh answered that question this way: "We took care of that with a good scrubbing on Saturday night."

It could be uncomfortable on winter days, especially if your seat was not near the stove. When I asked Marie about keeping warm, she said: "Well, if you must know, we girls wore long-handled underwear. On top of that we had sateen bloomers, then an under skirt, usually of dark-colored flannel, and then a heavy wool dress made out of somebody else's clothes. This was followed with big, heavy stockings above the knees, laced-up shoes until the eighth grade, then we graduated to low shoes." Marie was wearing enough clothes to share with several of today's teenagers even in cold weather.

When I asked Marie and Betty if there was anything they disliked about the Blose School, Betty said immediately: "The outhouse frightened me, the floor was too flimsy." Somebody accompanied Betty to the outhouse until she overcame her fear.

Behind every church, home and schoolhouse stood a building most people called the "outhouse." Following are two of five verses from a poem telling about this special building:

When memory keeps me company and moves to smiles or tears,

A weather-beaten object looms through the mist of years.

Behind the house and barn it stood a half a mile or more,

And hurrying feet a path made straight to its swinging door.

Its architecture was a type of simple classic art,

But in the tragedy of life, it played a leading part.

And oft the passing traveler drove slow and heaved a sigh,

To see the modest hired girl slip out with glances shy.

When grandpa had to "go out back" and make his morning call,

We'd bundle up the dear old man with muffler and a shawl.

I knew the hole on which he sat – 'twas padded all around,

And once I dared to sit there – 'twas all too wide I found.

My loins were all too little and I jackknifed there to stay,

They had to come and get me out, or I'd have passed away.

Then father said ambition was a thing that boys should shun,

And I just used the children's hole 'til childhood days were done.

Some attributed the poem to James Whitcomb Riley, but he denied writing it. I don't believe Riley did write that piece of poetry. He was enough of a rural person to know that "half a mile or more" was too far to walk on a cold, winter night.

I found a common thread running through everybody's memories of the one-room school. Their strongest feelings had nothing to do with subjects like arithmetic, reading or writing. Sometimes with misty eyes, but always with conviction, they used words like sharing, tolerance, family, camaraderie and community. The one-room school may truly have been a " temple of knowledge."

# How They Lived

They lived simple lives without ceremony. They didn't have the money to live any other way.

Recently we went to a wedding where the reception must have cost several thousand dollars. These were middle-class Americans. Like many in their day, my mother and father were married before a justice of the peace with no reception. Interestingly, the no-frills weddings of their day resulted in fewer divorces.

Unfortunately, there were times when the need to work won out over getting an education. Some highly qualified students had to stay home and work instead of continuing their education. The year Uncle Monroe took his eighth-grade examination, he scored second highest in Indiana County. Yet, he had to drop out of high school and go to work in the coal mine. To Uncle

Monroe and Aunt Jennie's credit, their three children were all college graduates.

# MEDICINE

They lived before flu shots, antibiotics and Dr. Jonas Salk's polio vaccine. They rarely saw a doctor, and drug stores didn't exist in their part of the world.

Many health treatments were either folk or patent medicines, and they were plentiful. Sometimes I believe the effectiveness of these medicines was gauged by smell. The more offensive the odor, the more effective the medicine.

Ranking them by the offensive-odor test, asafetida has to go in first place. This was a popular folk medicine containing the gum resin of various plants, and pronounced "a general prophylactic against diseases." It was placed in a small bag and tied around the neck until spring. It kept people away, if not diseases.

I'm told Grandad once broke up an evangelistic church service when he put some asafetida on the coal stove that heated the church. The rank, offensive smell drove the people out of church and few souls were saved that night.

My ancestors held poultices in high regard for any ailment involving the throat or chest. The dictionary defines poultice as: "a soft, moist mass of bread, meal, clay or other adhesive substance, usually heated, spread on a cloth, and applied to warm, moisten or stimulate an aching or inflamed part of the body." My definition differs slightly. I would describe a poultice as a warm, greasy, oily, clammy, pungent mixture placed on the body and covered with a flannel cloth. I still squirm when I imagine that warm mess against my chest. I hated poultices. It was a great day when antibiotics were discovered. That did away with most poultices and saved more lives.

Teas brewed from sassafras bark, boneset and horsetail plants were used as tonics to treat colds and fever.

One of the most famous of all patent medicines was Lydia Pinkam's Vegetable Compound. It was a popular cure-all for so-called "female complaints." The fact that it was 18 percent alcohol probably helped ease the pain. Even though Lydia died in 1883, the family knew she had a good thing going and continued the business into the 1960s. They even added Lydia Pinkam's Pink Pills which became a good seller.

Peddlers often came through the valley with a variety of household products and elixirs that would cure all ailments known to mankind. The Watkins man came most often, and had the greatest variety of home products and patent medicines. Every home had a bottle of Watkins Vanilla in the kitchen cupboard. Even so, the peddler I looked forward to seeing most was the one who sold Porter's Pain King Liniment and Salve. These two products were used on both man and animal. The salve was cream- colored and had its very own peculiar medical smell you knew would heal anything from sores on a cow's udder to a cut on a boy's foot. Even after all these years, if someone were to place a can of that salve under my nose, I believe I could identify the smell. Then the liniment was equally good on both horse and human.

There were a few during their lifetimes who never saw the inside of a hospital or a doctor's office. Grandad's only visit to a hospital came when bees stung his horses while making hay. Dick and Prince took off, dragging him behind them for some distance. He had all sorts of abrasions over most of his body.

Most people were born at home and died at home. I heard my sister's first cry when she came into this world; also, we were there when our brother, Jimmy, died. When Dad came into our bedroom, his very words were, "Jesus took Jimmy to Heaven last night." He died of pneumonia before antibiotics were discovered. Like many, he died before one of medicine's miracles was available.

One had a more-intimate association with both life and death while living on a farm before the burst of technology in the middle of the 20th century. I'm reminded of lines from Edgar Guest's poem, "Home."

Within the walls there's got t' be some babies born ... An' watch beside a loved one's bed, an' know that death is nigh ... It takes a heap o' living in a house t' make it home."

## F O O D

Water was steaming in the big, cast-iron kettle over an open fire, knives were sharpened, and Grandad had his rifle ready. It was a 22 Special, and packed a little more wallop than the regular 22 rifle.

It was time to butcher hogs. This was a very important day, providing most of the year's meat supply. The first hog was let out of the pen, and Grandad put it down with one shot between the eyes. Dead-eye John Lee Blose, hog-slayer and chief engineer of the day's events.

That first hog carcass soon went through an amazing transformation. The once-hairy animal was now a gleaming, ivory-colored carcass suspended in the air. It got that way by being sloshed around in a steel barrel of scalding water, then all the hair removed with special scrapers. Most of this was man's work. Any boy with common sense knew to stay out of the way.

Soon, the suspended carcass was separated into major cuts, such as hams, bacon, etc. First Grandad did something I've seen nobody else do. He would take a sharp axe (His tools were all sharp) and split the hog carcass down through the very middle of the backbone. Other people would need a saw for this operation.

Hams, shoulders and bacon would be put into a salt brine for curing. After the right number of days had passed, these cuts would be hung in the smokehouse. Smoking helped a little in preservation, but this step was done mostly for flavor. A fire was built in a sturdy, open container. Not any wood would do. Green apple and hickory were preferred. Green wood would smoke and smolder a long time with apple or hickory giving a richer flavor and smell. Pine and hemlock were unacceptable, with their high resin content. The smokehouse with its cuts of smoked meat was one of my favorite rural smells, right along with new-mown hay.

The big, cast-iron kettle had another important role besides heating water. As the carcasses were cut up, the heart, liver, tongue and other pieces of meat went into the large kettle until completely cooked. This large cauldron of cooked meat was visited often. A piece of meat was speared, salted and relished by hungry helpers, definitely including boys. What remained would later become the basis of liver pudding and scrapple.

When darkness came, activities moved to the house. It was time to grind all the fresh trimmings into sausage.

In the morning, there would be a special treat: fresh sausage and buckwheat cakes. These were old-fashion cakes made with pure buckwheat flour and yeast started at least the day before.

Buckwheat cakes have almost disappeared from the American menu. Yet, especially during the winter months, buckwheat cakes and sausage were staples in Blose Hollow. Not only was buckwheat a source of flour for the table, it was a common livestock feed, and one of the beekeepers' best nectar-producing plants. When buckwheat was in bloom, Uncle Harry's bees produced a deep, dark honey. I expect it would be considered a good antioxidant food in today's health-conscious society. Buckwheat had the advantage of maturing in only 10 to 12 weeks, and did better than most crops on thin, stony soil.

In 1918, Indiana County was the fourth-highest producer of buckwheat in the United States. Then in 1924, the nearby Marion Center Milling Company was the largest buckwheat grinding mill in Pennsylvania. That same year, the mill had an order from A&P Stores for 12,000 five-pound bags of buckwheat flour. Many of those acres that once grew buckwheat are now covered in Christmas trees.

For those wanting to try old-fashion buckwheat cakes, here's a recipe courtesy Zanella Milling Co., West Sunbury, Pa.:

Combine the following ingredients (Zanella suggests using an earthenware crock):

> 2 cups sour milk or buttermilk
> 1 teaspoon salt
> 1 tablespoon molasses
> 1/2 cake compressed yeast dissolved in water
> Add enough pure buckwheat flour to make a thick batter.
> Put in a warm place overnight.
> In the morning, add 1/2 teaspoon baking soda dissolved in water.
> If the batter is too thick, thin with water.
> Cook on a hot, greased griddle. Turn only once.
> Save a little of the batter and put in the refrigerator. Use this batter as a starter – no more yeast is needed.

I tried making them, and met with failure. Even though the griddle was well greased, the buckwheat cakes stuck to it like glue. After consulting several cookbooks, I can recommend adding at least three tablespoons of melted butter or cooking oil to the batter before placing it on the griddle. One of the cookbooks I consulted was published by the Pennsylvania State Grange. I could find no publication date or any other date mentioned in the entire book. Something interesting I did find was a poem they included from the very first Pennsylvania Grange Cookbook. I thought it had a connection to my search for a buckwheat cake recipe. It went like this:

> Of course, I'll gladly gib de rule
> I make beat biscuits by.
> Tho' I ain't so sure dat you can make
> Dem just the same as I.
> 'Case cookin's like religion is,
> Some's 'lected and some ain't
> An' rules don't know more make a cook
> Den sermons make a saint.

*from the First Pennsylvania Grange Cook Book*

I'm sure the first Grange cookbook was published many years ago, perhaps even when my grandmother was turning buckwheat cakes on her coal stove that Uncle Revere loved so much. Grandma and Grandad both belonged to the Grange in Wilgus, and the Grange in those days was much stronger than it is today. One of the things I found interesting was that women were allowed to vote within the Grange many years before they were allowed to vote in local, state or national elections.

A variety of toppings can be put on buckwheat cakes. One often used in Blose Hollow was "hog honey," a term I believe was coined by Uncle Monroe. This is nothing more than the skillet drippings from fried ham or bacon usually diluted with a bit of water. It is rich in flavor but would not make today's list of foods for a healthy heart.

Sausage making took place in the basement. A small barrel of cider from Uncle Walter's cider press usually appeared there in the fall. I'm not sure if the primary purpose of the cider was vinegar at a later date or hard cider before it turned to vinegar. I do know that near the barrel was a long, hollow, dry stem of Joe-Pye-weed. The hollow stem had one purpose: The siphoning of cider, preferably hard, by Grandad for his personal enjoyment. I suppose he knew there were others who helped themselves to that cider – preferably hard.

Food was plain and simple, but tasty and loaded with calories. It was suited to those working in the woods, on the farm or in the mines. The staples were things such as potatoes, homemade bread and butter, pork, and beans of all kinds — either baked or soup beans with a piece of pork. A big garden supplied much of the food during the summer.

Grandad and I ate lots of beans when I visited him after Grandma died and Uncle Revere was in the Army. Most of the time it was navy bean soup with a piece of pork fat. I still enjoy them. All it takes is some dried beans, a can of chicken broth and an onion.

Cooking was done on a coal stove. It also heated water for whatever purpose hot water was needed for. This even included washing clothes and taking a bath. Saturday night was bath night, and it was done in a zinc tub in the middle of the kitchen floor. It was impractical to change water after each person bathed, so it was nice to be first. That often involved some concessions and deals being made.

That coal stove was the object of both scorn and affection. Some, like my daughter, Susan, hated it. When the inexperienced put coal on the fire, black smoke would sometimes pour out into the kitchen. Over the years, smoke had given the kitchen and some other rooms a color darker than the original. Some could not accept this.

Uncle Revere was one who had a great affection for the coal stove. Maybe it had something to do with his spending hours and hours cutting kindling wood to fire up the stove in the morning. Uncle Revere was a bachelor who married later in life than usual. He and his new wife were making some changes and apparently had discussed the future of the coal stove. He said to his brother, Monroe, that the coal stove was going to stay because it "was the heart of the home." One morning shortly after that, Uncle Monroe, who lived across the road, called to his wife and said: "Come here, Jennie. The heart of the home is going out the back door." The walls were scrubbed down and the coal stove, however much nostalgia surrounded it, became a part of history.

## SOCIAL LIFE AND CELEBRATIONS

Much of their social life centered around the home and Blose School just across the road. The big event of the year was the school reunion. It was held in a grove of trees near the school, and people came early and stayed late. Most came on foot, some by horse and buggy, and a few in Model-T Fords. It was a family affair, many having no connection with the school. They came to visit and renew old acquaintances. Marshall Hamilton, a teacher at Blose School, sold pop for five cents a bottle. Five cents for a bottle of pop was the only money some of us had to spend. A crude stage was constructed in the middle of the grove where youngsters with budding musical talents would make their parents proud when they sang songs, usually hymns. Then there were adult performers of varying talent, often with a banjo and guitar or two. My brother Tom remembers them singing "Cowboy Jack," a popular song at the time.

After some searching, I found a copy of the song and it turned out to be a very sad cowboy ballad, probably written shortly after the Civil War. Jack was a lonely cowboy who leaves his sweetheart when a quarrel comes between them. Time passes and Jack learns that with her last breath "She breathed her sweetheart's name." Jack found her grave out on the lonely prairie, and the last of nine verses goes like this:

"Your sweetheart waits for you, Jack
  Your sweetheart waits for you
 Out on the lonely prairie
 Where the skies are always blue."

When it was time to eat, blankets were spread under the trees, Two things I could always count on were fried chicken and baked beans. Both, especially the chicken, were unlike today's picnic food.

Very, very early in the day, two barnyard hens or roosters would meet their ends, feathers plucked, birds cleaned, and then boiled until they were tender. With the old barnyard birds, this took a while, quite unlike Kentucky Fried Chicken broilers. After boiling, the pieces were coated with flour and seasoning, then browned in a big, black skillet on the coal stove. The final product was country fried chicken at its best. Preparing beans was a similar process. You had to start from scratch with dried beans the night before. There were no shortcuts, like getting beans out of a can. Food preparation started and ended at home.

Erma Gearhart, the 103-year-old, said she "enjoyed going to Lee Blose's for ice cream parties." I expect my grandparents' home was a center of activity as they lived next to the school and had four children who were students there.

My brother Tom gives this account of making ice cream:

"Since there were no refrigerators, perishable food was either canned or cured with enough salt to inhibit bacterial growth or it was dried. Since the farm had an icehouse, we would occasionally make ice cream – depending on the milk supply. Making ice cream, especially in the summer, was a treat everyone looked forward to. Uncle Walter, who lived on the next farm up the road, had a dam. It's now completely filled with silt, and it takes a keen eye to see that a body of water ever existed there. In the winter, it was customary to cut ice from the dam and haul it to the icehouse. The icehouse was nothing more than a shed over a pit dug in the ground. The pit and much of the shed over it was full of sawdust. The sawdust provided the insulation needed to keep the ice from melting too fast during warm weather. But it still melted and usually was gone by the end of summer –

or even before if there was not a good supply of ice laid in the previous winter.

"We had a six quart ice cream freezer, and Mom or Grandma would mix in about a gallon of milk or light cream and the other necessary ingredients to produce ice cream. I always volunteered to crank the freezer. Before that took place, though, we had to get a chunk of ice from the icehouse and wipe the sawdust off and then put it into a burlap bag. With a heavy hammer, we would proceed to smash the ice into small enough pieces so that it could be poured into the freezer. Of course, to the ice you had to add salt so that the brine would freeze the ice cream. The initial cranking was always easy. As the ice cream began to stiffen, it took more and more power to turn the crank. It was never appropriate, at least to me, to admit you were getting tired no matter how much your arm ached trying to turn that crank handle. Finally, someone in authority would say, "I think it's done." What a relief. But it was always worth the effort because you could usually look forward to getting your fill of ice cream – unless the number of visitors was extra large."

Fourth of July was a holiday celebrated with enthusiasm in Blose Hollow. Grandad had a cannon made to celebrate the day properly. He located a well-driller's bit and had one end welded shut. The bit was a very heavy piece of steel, approximately two-and-one-half- to three-feet long. Near the closed end, a small hole was drilled into the cavity. A squib or fuse was placed in the hole, followed by a charge of gunpowder that was put into the open end of the cannon. The next step was tamping several wads of dry paper against the gunpowder. This was followed by almost filling the bore of the cannon with moist earth, and tamping it down. With the cannon securely positioned against a tree stump, the fuse was lit and everybody ran for cover. Soon there would be an explosion reverberating through the valley and over the hills. People knew that John Lee Blose was at it again, this time celebrating Independence Day. Grandad's cannon would be no match for today's grand displays of fireworks. His enthusiasm was another matter. Unfortunately, the biggest use of our national holiday these days is as a vehicle for selling merchandise.

We duplicated Grandad's cannon in miniature using a sturdy tin can that had a push-on, pull-off lid. First, we put a nail hole in the closed end of the can, then added a small amount of carbide with even a smaller amount of water. We secured the lid and placed the can on the ground, clamping it down with a foot. We held a match to the nail hole to ignite the carbide gas that was forming in the can. Soon there was an explosion driving the lid helter-skelter through the air. Obviously, it was important to keep your foot firmly on the can. This was our substitute for firecrackers on the Fourth of July.

Because no one had the means of transportation we have today, most social activities took place at home or nearby. Things like cake walks, pie socials and even spelling bees drew many people to the Blose School.

## PRINTED MATERIAL

They may not have recognized the names Aaron Montgomery Ward or Richard Sears and Alvah Roebuck, but the people in Blose Hollow and all of rural America loved their catalogs. Ward's first catalog was a single sheet of paper in 1872. By 1904, the Mongomery Ward and Sears-Roebuck catalogs weighed four pounds each. People of the 21st century will never know the influence these two catalogs had on rural America in the early 1900s. They were fondly referred to as the "Farmer's Bible" and the "Nation's Wish Book." Thick as the Bible and almost as popular, these two catalogs were wish books for toys, new dresses, home furnishings, guns, farm tools and hundreds of things never before dreamed of. Thanks to parcel post and rural free delivery, main street U.S.A. came to Blose Hollow. In 1925, Sears-Roebuck alone sold 243 million dollars worth of goods, more than 95 percent of it by mail. The story is told about the farm boy whose Sunday school teacher asked him where the Ten Commandments came from. Without hesitation, he replied "The Sears-Roebuck catalog." Old editions were recycled in the outhouse. The catalogs had two kinds of paper: thin, flimsy pages and slick, smooth pages. The thin, flimsy pages were favored.

Magazines and newspapers were rare, except for the "Pennsylvania Grit" on occasion. This was a weekly newspaper with the word Grit always in big, bold letters at the top center of the first page. Because my wife's grandfather read the Grit, and published a weekly newspaper of his own in McConnellsburg, Pa., I considered that a good recommendation. The Grit, published in Williamsport, must have had a great circulation. It was really a family newspaper with something for everyone. It even had serial stories that continued from one edition to the next.

# THE RADIO

Listening to the news was almost a religion with Grandad. He would say "Let's get some fresh news," and on would go the radio, always tuned to KDKA Pittsburgh, the world's first commercial radio station. It was probably the only station to reach Blose Hollow in those days.

His favorite news reporter was Lowell Thomas, one of the greatest names of all time in radio news. Thomas traveled the world and spoke with a voice of authority. He started every broadcast saying "Good evening, everybody," and ended with "So long until tomorrow." His newscasting career spanned 50 years, and he was inducted into the Radio Hall of Fame in 1989.

Gabriel Heeter, another news reporter Grandad listened to, was always upbeat. However gloomy the world situation, Heeter would find something good to talk about, starting every broadcast with "Ah, yes, I've got good news tonight."

A radio program never missed was "Amos and Andy," a comedy about the antics of two black men and their friends. First airing in 1928, the show became the longest-running radio program in broadcast history. Eventually, it became a TV program but didn't last long. Times were changing and programs like "Amos and Andy" were considered too insulting and demeaning.

## Ku Klux Klan

In 1915, there was a rebirth of the Ku Klux Klan (KKK) and it reached into Blose Hollow. At least two family members were caught up in a movement that attracted thousands from Indiana County.

The KKK was founded in Polaski, Tenn., in 1866. Their first leader, called the Imperial Wizard, was the famous Confederate general, Nathan Bedford Forest.

The hooded Klansmen in their white robes became known for terrorizing and killing blacks in the South. To his credit, Forest soon left the KKK because of the extreme violence.

The following information on the KKK in Indiana County comes from Volume II of Stephenson's Indiana County History.

The KKK movement was very strong in Indiana County during the 1920s. One of the largest Klan meetings ever held in western Pennsylvania was on Saturday, July 18, 1924, in the nearby village of Cookport with 50,000 people attending. The local movement had little to do with blacks. It was primarily anti-foreign and anti-Catholic. One of their main activities was supporting white, Anglo-Saxon Protestants running for political office. Also, hooded Klan members attended Protestant church services and made generous donations. The "Indiana Weekly Messenger," a newspaper published in Indiana, was supportive of Klan activities.

Before long, the KKK built a 60-by-120-foot brick headquarters a few miles south of Indiana. Just before the building was to be dedicated, it was destroyed by an incendiary bomb. Catholic coal miners from the nearby town of Lucerne were suspected of setting off the explosion. Those responsible were never apprehended.

The Klan in Indiana County and Blose Hollow collapsed about as quickly as it rose to prominence. All that remains is one very old, hooded robe. All I will say is that it was not worn by my grandfather. The person to whom it belonged was a good man caught up in the fever of the times.

## A Church Remembered

My grandparents were not church-going people when I knew them. Yet, my cousin Ikey said on Sunday morning, Grandma would often put on a straw bonnet and off they would go to the Montgomery Church of the Brethren. That was a good walk, up and over the Boorbaugh, then down into Grant Township. When I knew Grandma, I don't believe she could have walked that far. They did not have an automobile. Few people did in those days.

I expect some church people considered Grandad a bit irreverent. To me, his religion was close to that of the American Indian. He had a great respect for the land. On occasion he would mention the "Great Spirit," and would often say "The earth is my mother, and on her bosom I will repose."

There was no doubt about my mother or father. They were faithful to their church. They attended regularly and expected their children to do the same.

My mother had an especially strong belief about baptism. She knew that Jesus walked into the River Jordan, and John the Baptist put him under the water three times: Once for the father, once for the Son, and once for the Holy Ghost. Anything less than that and you are only fooling yourself. Mom was truly a good and faithful member of the Church of the Brethren. After being immersed three times during baptism, it's easy to see why members of her church are called "Dunkards."

There is a church and a hymn that belong together. As my mind races back across the years I see a "... church in the valley by the wildwood, no lovelier spot in the dale; no place so dear to my childhood as the little white church in the vale." In my mind's eye, nothing suits Dr. William Pitt's hymn "The Church in the Wildwood" so much as the Montgomery Church of the Brethren.

How sweet it was on a clear summer morning to set out from out grandparents' home on that long walk to church. First though, we had to stop and check on the fish in the stream that meandered through the valley.

We needed to be careful where we stepped, and couldn't tarry long or we would be late for Sunday school.

Next, and off to the right, was George Colgan's place. If we didn't see George, chances are he was underground working in his coal mine. I'm not sure if George really separated the different days of the week. He heard the beat of a different drummer.

Part way up the hill we passed Obe Gromley's blacksmith shop. What a fascinating place this was for a boy: black smoke from some of George Colgan's coal, hammer against anvil, sparks flying from a red-hot horseshoe, and then Obe picking up the heavy foot of a draft horse and fitting the shoe. But that would have to wait until another day. Obe's shop was quiet today. It was Sunday.

Next, and farther up the hill, came John Small's farm. Chances are, he was already at church. You see, John was the Sunday school superintendent, and needed to be early – or at least on time.

How glad we were to reach the top, because from here it was all downhill to the church in the wildwood.

Grandad called that hilltop "the Boorbaugh." For him, it must have had a German meaning. In the right season, we would stop and pick some wild huckleberries. I know of no other place where they grew so big, so sweet and so plentiful.

We must hurry now or we would miss John Small's opening song. Late or not, we had one more stop to make. That was for a drink of cool, fresh water from a spring behind the church. Everyone used the same tin cup. There was little that was disposable in those days.

There were many wonderful, down-to-earth people who were part of the Montgomery Church of the Brethren. It was common for them to respectfully greet or address each other as "sister" or "brother." There was one who has a very special place in my memory. That person was Rev. Ivan Fetterman. Those who were part of that country church were truly blessed to have had that scholarly man of faith and wisdom among them. He was not only an outstanding minister but one who lived a life of kindness and compassion. I feel privileged to have known him.

Well over 60 years have passed since walking up that hill and then down to the church in the valley. Being a part of the Montgomery Church of the Brethren is a heritage to be treasured. I'm sure those who have passed on would share the sentiment expressed in the last verse of Dr. Pitt's hymn: "From the church in the valley by the wildwood, when day fades away into night, I would fain from this spot of my childhood wing my way home to the mansions of Light."

*Pencil Drawing — Grandad's Front Porch: My sincere thanks to Zarah Blair for the pencil drawing of Grandad's Front Porch. For better or worse, several Blose descendants had a hand in making alterations to this drawing.*

*Blanket Hill historical marker located along U.S. 422, Kittanning Township, Armstrong County, PA. About 1880, my great-grandparents, Michael Blose and his wife, Susanna, gathered their six children along with what meager possessions they had and moved to Montgomery Township in nearby Indiana County. There they settled in a valley that became known as "Blose Hollow." Today there are roads officially designated as Blose Road at both locations. I came to Armstrong County in 1955 as an agricultural agent with the Penn State University Extension Service. It was then I first learned my great-great-granparents lived in Armstrong County and are buried in Christ Lutheran Church Cemetery, Kittanning Township.*

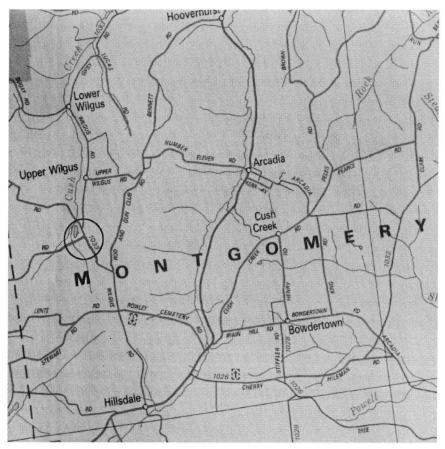

*Offical 2005 Pendot Highway Map, Indiana County, PA. The center of Blose Hollow is where Blose Road meets Wilgus Road — shown here in the circled area.*

*The four sons of Michael Jr. and Susanna Blose. My mother said this picture was taken about 1912 in Saxonburg, PA, when the four brothers went to visit their deceased mother's sister, Aunt Maggie Dugan. Left to Right: George Francis "Frank," Walter Michael, James Henry "Harry," and John Lee. Judging from their dress it must have been a very special ocassion. All wore white shirts, bow ties, and note those bowler hats! This was not the usual Blose Hollow look.*

*Front Porch Veterans — A gathering at the front porch in 1948. Uncle Revere, sitting on the swing, is back from the South Pacific and World War II. He is once again teaching school. Many who once gathered on the porch have left for far off places to earn a living, some are in college, thanks to the GI Bill, and sadly, some have passed on. Three are sitting on the porch deck in much the same manner as in past years but never in such deep contemplation. Left to right are Johnny Irwin, Grandad, and Henry Gromley. Johnny and Henry never married. They were good men who worked hard and drank too much. That didn't help them in their final years. Grandad lived to be 90, outliving Grandma by 22 years.*

*The Blose School 1887-1936. The one-room school would fall far short of meeting our expectations in the twenty-first century. They were without plumbing, custodians, snow days, sick days for teachers, school nurses, indoor restrooms, electricity, school buses, teacher tenure, cafeterias, auditoriums, principals and most everything else we take for granted. In spite of all this, these primitive looking buildings filled an educational void in the lives of people living in rual America, They were once proudly referred to as "Temples of Knowledge." This simple looking building played a very important role in the social as well as educational lives of all those living in Blose Hollow.*

*The Blose School Bell. The bell that once called the students to class now sits on a special pedestal below the old school house. The bell is special because there is a piece missing. This happened when the Armistice was signed at the end of World War I. The people in Blose Hollow rang the bell so long and so enthusiastically that a piece fell out. Imagine what a celebration that must have been.*

*Blose School Class of 1892* — Whoever took this picture over one hundred years ago certainly positioned the students so that all could be seen. All were students except the two men standing in the doorway. The man on the left is the teacher; my great-uncle Walter Blose. To his left is his father, Michael Blose, Jr. Walter was the first of many teachers among the descendants of Michael and Susanna Blose. The young man on the extreme left wearing suspenders is my grandfather, John Lee Blose. Walter also had his sister Sadie and brother Harry as students. All the people in this picture were Anglo-Saxon. This would change in the early 1900s when immigrants from Eastern Europe came to work in the coal mines at Wilgus. This happened throughout the entire Appalachian region creating a great melting pot of people and ideas.

*Sarah Lucretia Blose*
*Country School Teacher*

*She started teaching at 18 years of age after two years at the Indiana Normal School located in Indiana, PA. In the early 1900's, hundreds of young men and women were graduated from this school and destined to take on the challenge of teaching in the one-room schools scattered across Pennsylvania. The Indiana Normal School would later become Indiana State Teachers College and eventually Indiana University of Pennsylvania.*

*Sarah Lucretia's first teaching assignment was in the village of Gypsy, Montgomery Township, Indiana County, PA. This was two miles from her home and she was lucky to be able to ride in the horse and buggy with her Uncle Walter, who also taught in Gypsy. I'll bet she learned a lot in those buggy rides because her uncle was an excellent teacher.*

*In her second year of teaching she was assigned to the Brickell School in Lower Wilgus where there were 77 students. Can you imagine a nineteen year-old today being placed in a room with 77 students of all ages. Sarah Lucretia was essentially on her own. She was the teacher and also the principal, nurse, head custodian, athletic director and whatever else needed done. There was an additional challenge in Lower Wilgus. Many of the students were children of immigrant coal miners from Eastern Europe and Italy and did not speak English. What an educational challenge that must have been! I expect Sarah Lucretia learned more than the students.*

*Sarah Lucretia's teaching career ended in 1925 when she met Thomas King. They were married and "married ladies" were frowned upon by the school directors. Sometime later I became the second son of Sarah Lucretia. Three things she was proudest of in her life were: 1. Her family, 2. Her church and 3. Her time teaching in the rural one-room schools. She was the guiding force in our family.*

*I wonder why those boys appear to be in such good humor? Maybe it was a trick they played on an unsuspecting student in the outhouse, that small building hidden behind the tree. It must have been something special because film and cameras weren't too plentiful when this picture was taken. We believe the boy in the middle is Monroe Blose, born in 1905, so you can guess when the picture might have been taken. In the background note the rail fence in need of repair, the Blose School, and the home of my grandparents, John Lee and Amanda Pearl Blose. This home was completely destroyed by fire and Grandad built another one on the same location.*

*Walter Michael Blose and Mary Alice Bennett*
*Married December 21, 1895*

*John Lee Blose and Amanda Pearl Shaffer*
*Married January 1, 1901*

*Sara Anna, "Aunt Sadie," was the youngest child of Michael Jr. and Susanna Blose. She married John C. Irwin in 1896. Their home was a farm on top of the hill going east out of Blose Hollow. Two things come to my mind when I think of their farm. First, they had the biggest and best barn in all of Montgomery Township. Second, they had the stoniest farm in the entire township. They spent a lifetime gathering stones. Most of them went to build the highest and widest stone fences I've ever seen. I do not have a picture of Aunt Sadie and Uncle John. John Irwin was taller than the Bloses. Like Grandad, he carried no extra weight. He spent a lifetime wrestling a living out of stony land that would have challenged the best of us. They had three children: Josephine, John and Harry. For reasons best known to those who have passed on, their two sons left home, one never to return. It was a great tragedy, especially for Aunt Sadie to have a young son walk off the farm, never to return. Aunt Sadie and Uncle John both died in 1943 never knowing what happened to their son Harry. I write about John and his brother Harry in another part of this book.*

*A picture from the front porch of Walter and Molly Blose in 1900. Adults left to right: Harry Blose, Michael Blose Jr. (father of Harry, Walter and John Lee,) Walter Blose and wife Molly, Mrs. Bennett (Mollie's mother), and John Lee Blose. The two boys, James and Murray, are children of Walter and Molly. Harry never married, Michael Jr. died in 1910 at the age of 88. His wife, Susanna, died in 1891, four days before her 56th birthday. Walter died in 1934 while Molly, even though frail-looking in this picture, lived on to 1958. John Lee married Amanda Pearl Shaffer in 1901. The oldest boy, Murray, enlisted in the army during World War I. He was a victim of the flu epidemic that raged across the world in 1918 and was honorably discharged one year after enlising. Like other young men, James had a yearning to go west. He left Blose Hollow when a young man and settled in Drumright, Oklahoma, where he stayed and raised a family. Two of Michael Juniors children, Frank and Sadie, were married when this picture was taken and lived on nearby farms.*

*Riding the Hay Wagon — I can think of better things to do than hay making on
a hot July day. One thing I disliked most was bits of hay getting between my
shirt and sweaty skin. It became all too itchy. However, when the hay field
happened to be on top of the Boorbaugh, that made it worthwhile. It was a long
wagon ride up and something we all enjoyed, was the long ride home on top of
the hay wagon. Not many farmers would tolerate this many children trampling
hay on top of a wagon. We were all welcome on Grandad's wagon.*

*Grandad Harvesting Corn — Even in his waning years, Grandad would take his corn knife to the field. One by one, the corn stalks would be cut and shocked. Later it would be husked in the field or on the barn floor sometimes at a husking bee. This was when neighbors got together to have some fun while doing a chore. If a single man husked out a red ear he was entitled to kiss the girl of his choice. Of course there were refreshments often including apple cider from Uncle Walter's cider press. If the cider had become a little hard that was all the better. I've heard it said the wealthy celebrated with balls and the poor celebrated with bees. Machines put an end to husking bees. That's too bad. Sometimes I think technology will do us in. Note Grandad is wearing glasses. I was with him when he bought his glasses at G.C. Murphy Company Five and Ten in Indiana. Grandad tried on their selection of glasses until he found the pair that suited him best.*

*Grain Cradle — My brother Fred with Grandad's grain cradle. The cradle was used to harvest small grain like oats, wheat, rye and barley. It was a pleasure watching Grandad move back and forth across a field cutting grain and laying it down in a swath. Every bit like a well-trained athlete, it took skill and stamina to do the cradling hour after hour. Small wonder that all his life he was little more that muscle, bone and sinew.*

*Frank and Maggie Blose — Frank was the oldest child of Michael and Susanna Blose. He and Magdaline Buchanan, "Aunt Maggie," were married on March 21, 1909. Maggie was his second wife and they had three children. Uncle Frank and his first wife, Amanda, had seven children, Amanda died in 1905 and they are buried side by side in Rowley Cemetery. It was the custom in those days to be buried beside your first spouse. True to that custom, Aunt Maggie is buried beside her first spouse, Joseph Buchanan, in Montgomery Cemetery. What would they have done had Aunt Maggie not had a first husband? I hope she would have been in at least the same burial plot as Frank and Amanda.*

*Thomas and Sarah Lucretia King — My parents, Thomas and Sarah Lucretia King, were married on June 24, 1925, sixteen years after Uncle Frank and Aunt Maggie. What do these two bride and groom pictures have in common? Of course, the groom is sitting and the bride is standing. All the wedding pictures I've seen from this era were like these two. How do they differ? In just 16 years ladies' dresses got shorter. The hemline has gone well above my mother's ankles. Her arms are bare too. The mustache and bow tie are also gone. Wedding pictures were quite unlike today. The wedding was usually a private affair and later the bride and groom went to have their picture taken.*

*Henry Ford's Model T — Henry Ford changed America when he introduced his Model-T early in the Twentieth Century. With today's car prices, it's hard to believe at one point Ford's car cost as little as $290. He said "People could have any color they wanted as long as it was black." Dirt roads were fine for horses but not Henry Ford's new "Tin Lizzie." Every spring Grandad could count on hitching up his team and pulling somebody's car out of the mud. In 1930 Gifford Pinchot ran for governor of Pennsylvania promising to take people out of the mud. Pinchot won easily. In Pennsylvania the new blacktop roads became known as "Pinchot Roads."*

*The Homestead — My grandparent's home today. The front porch I knew as a boy is gone. It disappeared shortly after Uncle Revere got married. That disappearance put an abrupt end to those front porch gatherings I enjoyed so much when I was growing up. The Blose School still stands on the right and is hidden by several tall, columnar arborvitae. Directly behind the house on the distant hill is Grandad's mystical Boorbaugh where the spirits dwelled. The property is now owned and well-maintained by Mark Stebbins, great-great-grandson of Michael Jr. and Susanna Blose.*

*The author, Bill King, at three years of age in Blose Hollow.*

*Working Class Family in World War I — Whatever made my grandparent's family look so serious? I would like to know the story behind this picture. Unfortunately, all those who know have passed on. Front row, left to right: Uncle Monroe, Uncle Revere, Sarah Lucretia (my mother), Grandma and Grandad. In back are Uncle Richard and half-sister, Myra. My mother looks almost bellligerent. Long before I was born, Grandad worked in the Rochester and Pittsburgh coal mine at Wilgus. When the coal mine played out so did Wilgus. A stranger passing through today would never know there was once a thriving community here with homes, stores and even a skating rink. Wilgus is a town that has disappeared. The only other time I have seen the word Wilgus was on the side of a pickup truck in Cadiz, Ohio. The truck was going too fast for me to find out what it was about. I believe Wilgus was an Englishman who traded in the coal market.*

1965 Michael Jr. and Susanna Blose Reunion — 1965 marked the first Michael Jr. and Susanna Blose Reunion. There are thirteen of their grandchildren in this first reunion picture. Second row, left to right: 1st person - Lucy Blose Spicher, 4th person - Lucretia Blose King, 5th person - Betty Blose Mumau, 8th person - Josephine Irwin Roodhouse. Third row, left to right: 1st person - Mildred Blose Burns, 2nd person - Ethel Blose Catherman, 3rd person - Monroe Blose. Fourth row, left to right: 3rd person - Dean Blose, 7th person - Daisy Blose Tyger, 8th person - James Blose, 9th person - Foster Blose, 10th person - Marie Blose Rorabaugh. Fifth row, left to right: 4th person - Revere Blose. Michael Jr. and Susanna Blose had a total of 31 grandchildren.

*2005 Michael Jr. and Susanna Blose Reunion — Forty years have passed since that first reunion. Those who were in the front row of the first reunion picture are now married and have children. Four grandchildren of Michael and Susanna Blose are still living. Three are sitting in the second row; left to right: Marie Rorabaugh, June Gromley, and Betty Mumau, all sisters and children of Walter and Molly Blose. The three sisters received special recognition from President Beckie Blose. The fourth grandchild, Ethel Catherman, was unable to attend.*

*Montgomery Church of the Brethren — It was a long, long walk over a dirt road from my grandparent's home to the Montgomery Church of the Brethren. When this church comes to mind I always think of this hymn: "The Church in the Wildwood." It is a beautiful and poignant song I don't hear much anymore. The Church of the Brethren traces back to the 16th century in Germany. Two words come to mind when I think of this denomination: peace and dunkard. Devout members believe in peace and non-participation in war. Also, they have long been known as "Dunkards" because baptism is by full immersion three times in water: Once for the Father, once for the Son, and once for the Holy Ghost. This congregation has built a new church along a main highway a few miles away. It is no longer "The Church in the Wildwood."*

# THE FRONT PORCH

Grandad's front porch stretched across the front of the house and had no railing. Those who came simply hoisted their behinds up on the porch deck leaving their legs hang over the edge while they traded bits of information and told stories.

They came from several different directions; and all traveled on foot. These were men experienced in farming, cutting timber and working in the coal mines. Talk often centered around feats of strength and human endurance. Bragging rights belonged to those who cradled the most grain in a day, mined the most coal or cut the most timber.

They had their heroes, too. When I arrived at the front porch for the first time, those heroes included Franklin D. Roosevelt, newly elected president of the United States, and John L. Lewis, president of the United

Mine Workers of America (UMWA). Richard Custred, a friend who grew up in Sagamore, another Indiana County coal town, said many homes in Sagamore had three pictures hanging on the wall: Jesus Christ, President Roosevelt and John L. Lewis, but not necessarily in that order.

John L. Lewis was president of the UMWA for 40 years, from 1920 to 1960. Lewis, with his penetrating eyes, huge bushy eyebrows and great head of hair, was an eloquent, thunderous and combative spokesman for the miners. One of his famous statements to the miners was "I have pleaded your case, not in the tones of a feeble mendicant asking alms, but in the thundering voice of the captain of a mighty host ..."

My family could identify with the coal-mining song made popular by Tennessee Ernie Ford. Four lines I always remember go like this:

> "You load sixteen tons and what do you get?
> Another day older and deeper in debt.
> Saint Peter, don't you call me 'cause I can't go,
> I owe my soul to the company store."

One of my mother's main goals in life was to get enough cash ahead and leave the company store. She realized that goal, and I remember the day the transition was made to Sgriccia's Store in Clymer. My parents opened the account with Carbino Sgriccia and the event was celebrated with a grand treat – a bag of Hershey's Kisses.

As the son of a coal miner, I appreciate what Lewis did for miners in the early years. However, as a Navy veteran of World War II, I resented his calling the miners out on strike during the war years. Then, Lewis was not always consistent. He criticized President Roosevelt for seeking a third term while he continued on as president of the UMWA for an unprecedented 40 years.

Shortly after the war, he again called the miners out on strike. President Truman was against the strike because the country was recovering from the war and trying to rebuild Europe under the Marshall Plan. The president was granted an injunction barring the strike. In November 1946, Lewis attempted to see the president. Truman refused him an audience and said "The White House is open to anybody with legitimate business; but not to that son of a bitch." Lewis met his match in plain-spoken Harry S. Truman.

Once, after the war, I talked with Grandad about John L. Lewis. Grandad compared him to the Biblical Moses leading the children of Israel out of bondage in Egypt. Few labor leaders have been able to stir up passion and loyalty like John L. Lewis.

Coal mining had a great impact on the kind of people we are in America. Before 1900, we were pretty much an Anglo-Saxon nation. Eileen Mountjoy Cooper, writing about the coal industry in Indiana County, pointed out that in 1909, there were at least 29 deep mines in Montgomery Township alone. Coal companies needed workers for these mines and made a concerted effort to bring emigrant labor from eastern Europe and Italy. Their immigration program was successful. I have student rosters for the Blose School in 1892 and 1921. In 1892, the names are all Anglo-Saxon. In 1921, names like Bettino, Bruno, Gentillo, Goydich, Menosky and Petras appear on the roster. We had truly become a melting pot.

# BOXING

As with many major colleges and universities, Penn State had a boxing team when I was a student there after World War II. Today, there is little interest in boxing, and boxing teams are no longer part of the college sports program. Apparently they consider it too brutal.

Brutal or not, it was greatly enjoyed by those who gathered at Grandad's front porch. On the night of a boxing match, everybody gathered around the battery-operated radio with great suspense, waiting for the opening bell. There were three favorites, all heavyweights. First was Jack Demsey. They called him the "Manassa Mauler" after his hometown in Colorado and his style of fighting. Demsey demolished one boxer after another. After hanging up his gloves, he opened a restaurant and bar in New York City. After coming home from the war, Uncle Revere made a special trip to New York to meet the famous boxer. He met Demsey, and I believe it was a highlight of Uncle Revere's life.

After Demsey came Joe Lewis, a black man from Detroit, and Max Schmeling, a German. These two boxers captured the world's attention in the latter part of the 1930s. Schmeling's career as a boxer was on the rise at the same time Adolph Hitler, the Nazi dictator, was gaining power.

Joe Lewis and Max Schmeling faced each other twice in the boxing ring during their careers. They met first in 1936, when Schmeling knocked Lewis out in the 12th round. Their second fight was in 1938, in New York's Yankee Stadium. Lewis was the heavyweight champion at that time, and he was facing the only boxer who had ever defeated him. Tension was running high, and the whole world was watching, especially Hitler and his propaganda minister, Joseph Goebbels. They wanted a victory for Germany's Third Reich.

On the evening of the fight, everybody on Grandad's front porch moved into the living room and crowded round the battery-powered radio. Even through there was none in the house, electricity charged the atmosphere. This was no ordinary boxing match. It was America against Nazi Germany. Grandad's German ancestry meant nothing that night.

Lewis, whose nickname had become the "Brown Bomber," came to fight. He put Schmeling on the canvas at two minutes and four seconds into the first round. America was ecstatic and Germany was shocked. Needless to say, Schmeling fell out of favor with Hitler and the Nazi party. Schmeling's propaganda value hit bottom when Lewis knocked him out and he laid on the canvas.

Lewis was a winner in the boxing ring but a loser when it came to his personal finances. Ironically, one of the people who came to his rescue was Schmeling. Both men served in their countries' militaries during World War II. Lewis is buried at Arlington National Cemetery. Schmeling died on Feb. 2, 2005, at the age of 99. He would have been 100 on Sept. 28, 2005. Being knocked out in 1938 didn't affect his longevity.

# FREQUENT PORCH VISITORS

Uncle Harry was James Henry Blose, one of Grandad's three brothers. He lived in his parents' homestead, and like many who gathered at the front porch, was a bachelor.

Uncle Harry was the only snake collector I've ever known. His kind were black snakes that have been known to get as long as eight feet. Even though nonpoisonous, they were still feared by most people. If anybody was interested, he would gladly get a snake out of the large wooden box and allow it to crawl over his body. As a little boy I wondered if the snake was going to curl around his neck and choke Uncle Harry to death.

The story is told that Uncle Monroe, my grandparents' son, became very sickly when he was 5 or 6 years old.

None of the home remedies would cure his ailment. As time went on, he became very listless and they feared Uncle Monroe would not survive. One day, Mrs. Bennett, mother of Uncle Walter's wife, Mollie, stopped in for a visit. When leaving she said to Grandma "Monroe is under a spell put on him by Harry's snakes. For his own well-being, he must be taken away where he will not be affected." Uncle Monroe was taken to stay at Aunt Sadie's house. It was like a tonic. His health rapidly improved and he returned home after a few weeks. Once again his health went into a sharp decline. Something had to be done. On the first occasion Uncle Harry was away, Grandad built a huge fire and threw the snake box into the flames. That same night, Uncle Monroe was said to have slept the whole night through and was soon a healthy boy once again. Nothing was said about what might have happened between Grandad and Uncle Harry. I do know that some years later, he again took up collecting black snakes. Fortunately, my generation escaped coming under their evil spell.

Like many in the valley, Harry was a Democrat. How his sister, Sadie, ever became a Republican, I don't know. Maybe she was influenced by her husband, John Irwin. When Franklin D. Roosevelt was running against Alf Landon of Kansas for president in 1936, Aunt Sadie came to the election house wearing a large sunflower button because Kansas was known as the "Sunflower State." Uncle Harry was serving as judge of election. When he saw his sister with the big sunflower, he said "Sadie, that will be wilted like hell by evening. He was right. Roosevelt won with 60 percent of the popular vote.

What Erma Gearheart said about Uncle Harry was a typical reaction from those who knew him. (Erma was the 103-year-old I interviewed because she knew many of my ancestors.) Erma said she was attending a homemade ice cream party at my grandparents' home and everybody was expected to turn the ice cream freezer. When it came her turn, she had great difficulty because she was so tiny and the ice cream was beginning to freeze. Erma said "Harry Blose was such a nice man. He said 'Let me help you because the freezer is becoming hard to turn.' " That little act of kindness stayed with her almost 90 years.

Few people today have ever eaten comb honey. Uncle Harry was also a beekeeper and it was a real treat when he would give us a square of comb honey in a small wooden frame. Comb honey included beeswax along with the honey. After enjoying the liquid honey, you had a ball of wax to chew on for as long as you liked. Today, we buy liquid honey that has been extracted from the comb.

One summer day I quickly made my way to the shade of a cherry tree near Uncle Harry's house. My head was spinning and my stomach churning. This can happen to a young boy when he wants to act like a man. I decided I would try some of Uncle Harry's Cutty Pipe tobacco. This tobacco brand was in a class by itself. Cutty Pipe was extra strong, dark, stringy and multipurpose. You could chew it, roll it into cigarettes or smoke it in a pipe. The pipe smoke was especially rank. Any method was guaranteed to make a boy sick. Today, I expect the only place you can find a package of Cutty Pipe would be in a museum.

Uncle Revere was Paul Revere Blose, my grandparents' youngest child, and mathematics was his great passion in life. He not only taught mathematics, Uncle Revere worked on math problems wherever he went. There must be a strong math gene in the Blose line because there are several math teachers. Uncle Revere always had a math question to spring on his nephews and nieces. Too often, I had to dance around his question trying not to look too stupid. One day, to my great delight, he said "Billy, if you had a duck behind two ducks, a duck ahead of two ducks and a duck between two ducks, how many ducks would you have?" Would you believe my mother had asked us the same question a few days earlier? Anyway, I pretended to struggle with the duck question before giving Uncle Revere the answer. The person who could handle his math problems was my cousin, Carolyn Blose, who became a math teacher and still tutors students even after retirement. It was good to have her around when Uncle Revere showed up.

At Uncle Revere's funeral, there was an algebra book beneath his hands.

Uncle Revere and other young men were part of something unique in American coal towns during the 1920s and '30s. Uncle Revere and Henry Gromley, both part of the front porch group, played on a company-sponsored baseball team. Spectator interest was great, and competition was keen among coal towns of any size in western Pennsylvania. This cooperative community-company effort ended with World War II, when young men went off to war and the deep mines began to shut down. It wasn't long until entire towns were put on the market. The end of company coal towns also marked the end of a fascinating chapter in American history.

Automobiles were rare in those days, and rarer still in Blose Hollow. Uncle Revere was the only one of the front porch group to own a car. They were always second-hand and came from Pittsburgh. A new car was some years in the future. He would very often come to Clymer and take us to the farm. The car I liked best was a coupe with a rumble seat. Riding back there in the open air was something not many kids got to do.

Our family did not get a car until 1941. That was a gray 1935 Chevrolet sedan with a manual gear shift on the floor. The real test when learning to drive a car like that was starting out on a hill from a dead stop. One foot was on the clutch, one on the floor brake, one hand on the emergency brake and the other on the steering wheel. If all body parts did not work in sync, the car acted like a jackrabbit and the engine usually stalled. That headache ended with the automatic transmission.

A stream meandered through the valley below the school. It wasn't big, but still offered many hours of swimming and fishing. The fishing gear consisted of a good, sturdy tree branch, a piece of wrapping cord, and, when real fishing hooks weren't available, a straight pin bent into the form of a fishing hook. Bait was usually no problem because it's a poor barnyard that doesn't have a supply of nice fat fishing worms. Anything we caught was usually eaten along the stream bank: Fresh, smoked, charred fish at its best. I'll bet my mother and grandmother were glad they didn't have that mess in the house. If the fish weren't biting, frog legs went on the menu — roasted over an open fire just like the fish. Unfortunately, I never became a connoisseur of frog legs. The only place I've eaten them is along that stream in Blose Hollow. I do remember the flesh was white and about the texture of chicken; also the leg muscles would quiver and twitch as they roasted.

When Grandad died, Uncle Revere inherited the homestead and some adjoining acreage. He eliminated that stretch of the stream where we spent all those hours fishing and swimming. In it's place he put a small lake and pavilion. It's very nice for picnics and reunions, but the meandering stream offered more possibilities for kids.

Henry Gromley was the son of Obadiah "Obe" Gromley, a blacksmith and farmer who lived on a farm joining George Colgan's place. I find it interesting how some ancient Biblical names have become popular. We have two grandsons with the names Benjamin and Nathan, but Henry's father is the only person I've known with the name Obadiah. My brother Fred remembers Obe coming to Grandad's occasionally, but would sit on the embankment beside the road opposite the front porch and whittle wood. He was in famous company because Gen. Ulysses S. Grant liked to whittle wood. For what it's worth, I did learn that Obadiah is the shortest book in the Bible with only 21 verses.

Henry, like many who came to the front porch, was a bachelor. Unlike the others, he had only one eye.

During an early visit to the porch, I looked down at the porch deck and was shocked to see an eye looking up at me. It was Henry's glass eye. He had taken it out of his eye socket and placed it there for my benefit. I learned later a tree twig snapped back and ruined his eye while he was driving the cows to the barn for milking. Watching him do things, most people would never realize that Henry had only one eye.

Henry Gromley was one of the friendliest persons I've ever known, but he had a weakness shared by a few others in his day. Occasionally, Henry would go on a "bender." That's when you tip the bottle too long and too often. When one of these occurred, Henry would often show up at the back door for coffee and a confessional. Mom would serve him coffee and Henry, sometimes misty-eyed, would swear to my mother that from that day forward he was taking a new path never to drink again. He never succeeded in making the transition.

Henry played baseball with Uncle Revere on the Gypsy team. Once he was called on as a relief pitcher. Henry, with his one eye, won the baseball game. That victory triggered a bender that lasted for several days. Sad that success had to be handled that way.

Fate was not good to this kind and friendly man. Eventually his good eye failed and Henry became completely blind. He lived with a friend who was challenged to keep his own life in order, let alone two.

My brother Fred visited Henry before he died and said he was mentally alert, could still laugh, but lived in a "boar's nest." I think we failed this good man.

Barney Gromley was a nephew of Henry and one of the younger visitors to the front porch. Barney was usually quiet but would burst into song with little or no encouragement. I can still see his vocal chords stretching as he tried to get all he could out of "Tennessee Waltz." After singing a verse or two, off he would go, looking for a ride to the skating rink in Clymer. My sister, Carol Ann, said Barney was a wonderful skater, twirling around and going backward and forward at great speed. Barney was one of several from the valley who migrated to Erie, Pa. Barney followed the beat of a different drummer, and we lost touch with him.

George Colgan lived a short distance down the road from Grandad's place. When I knew him, he mined house coal for a living. The mine was on his property just a short distance from the back door.

George never had much use for soap and water. When he showed up at the front porch, he was usually in bib overalls sporting a full beard. If George had stepped out of his overalls I believe they would have stood on there own. George and his clothes would have made a great before-and-after soap commercial.

He possessed something the group respected, and that was brute strength. Uncle Revere said there was no stronger man in the community than George Colgan in his prime. He recalled seeing him hoist a 200 pound keg of spikes on his shoulder and carry it up two flights of steps at the mine tipple in Wilgus.

George always showed up at butchering time and special events like corn-husking bees. I remember a husking bee when he came late and the only food left was hot dogs. As a boy I sat by the fire and marveled at how a man with no teeth could make so many hot dogs disappear so fast. He never missed butchering time when the liver, heart, tongue and head meat were cooking in the big iron kettle.

When the meat was cooked, George would spear a chunk of meat, salt it liberally and down it would go with a smile on his face and an appreciative smack of the lips. George was a good man whose rough side was out.

Ted Koozer showed up at the front porch on occasion. Ted lived in one of the few houses left in the mining town of Wilgus. He was a person I pitied. Long before I knew him, he lost an arm in a mining accident. The empty sleeve he kept tucked under his belt. Ted was never too neat, but much of that probably came from living alone and needing to do things with only one arm. As a boy, I was fascinated watching him manage to do things with that lone arm and one set of fingers. When loading his pipe, he held it between his knees or in his mouth, then it was a long process of filling the pipe from a tin of Half and Half pipe tobacco. Nothing was easy.

My cousin, Tom Blose, tells about stopping at Ted's place when he had honey bees nesting between a partition in his house. When Ted wanted some honey, ignoring the bees, he would reach in through an opening, grab a handful of honey, and place it on a dish. He definitely bypassed a number of steps in the art of beekeeping.

When television arrived, the front porch group moved inside to watch some favorite programs. This was after Grandma died and while Uncle Revere was in the army. One evening, Uncle Monroe stopped for a visit while they were watching "The Lone Ranger." The Lone Ranger and Tonto were trapped in what seemed like an impossible situation. Uncle Monroe said in a way only he could "Well, that's the end of him." Ted signaled his disagreement by saying "Like hell, that's the Lone Ranger." They had great faith in their hero.

# WHISKEY

Small whiskey stills were plentiful throughout western Pennsylvania in the early years of our country. The main reason for this was a very practical one. Whiskey was the cheapest way of hauling corn and rye over the mountains to eastern markets. A pack-horse could carry 24 bushels of rye as whiskey but only four as grain.

Of course, there was plenty of whiskey that never reached the eastern market. Rev. Robert McCaslin, a Presbyterian, made some interesting comments while speaking during the 1887 Slate Lick Reunion. Slate Lick is a village in Armstrong County near where I live. The entire proceedings of an 1887 reunion were published in a wonderful little historical volume. It records that McCaslin said:

"So common was the drinking habit that whiskey came to be looked upon as a necessary beverage. Families were considered wanting in hospitality that did not offer it to their friends. It was sort of a ubiquitous spirit. It was the universal accompaniment of labor in every department. It was present in all harvest fields; it was an essential element of all frolics, it was at all "raisings," "log rollings,' "huskings," "sugar boilings." "scutchings," "sheep washings," and present at all sporting occasions. It was present on the occasion of a birth, a marriage, or a death and funeral. In winter it was used to keep people warm, and in the summer it was supposed to moderate the heat. In damp or wet weather, it prevented colds, and in sickly seasons it frowned down on all diseases. And so it was that everybody drank in the early days; ministers, and all the people; men and women, old and young. But there was not much more drunkenness then than now. The constant, active outdoor exercise and plain homely food, in great measure served to neutralize the intoxicating virus..."

Eventually the production and consumption of whiskey declined due to a strong temperance movement and better transportation methods for getting corn and rye to market. Still, there was a lingering desire for some spirits stronger than beer. Blose Hollow was not immune.

I am not a social worker or psychologist, and don't know why some people drink to the point of drunkenness. On occasion, a few in Blose Hollow did just that. They weren't habitual drunkards, but felt the need to "tie one on" from time to time. Grandad was one of those people, while his brother Walter could ignore whiskey completely.

The story is told that once Grandad had too much to drink and started waving his shotgun around. Only Grandma and Uncle Revere were present. Both were scared and neither could completely handle the situation. Uncle Revere went for his brother, Uncle Monroe, who was newly married and lived a half mile up the road. He went for the right person. Uncle Monroe possessed the temperament to defuse the situation. When he arrived, Grandad had taken up a position inside the barnyard gate and was shouting " I will wade blood up to my neck, but I'll never surrender my arms." This went on for a short time while Uncle Monroe reasoned with his father. It wasn't long until Grandad surrendered his arms.

This was the same man who told stories and laughed with us, who would take as many grandchildren who wanted to go up to the barn for a night in the haymow, who would allow all of us to ride on a load of hay from the Boorbaugh to the barn, the same man who on a hot day would search out a spring so his grandson could have a drink of cool water, and the same man who showed his pride when his grandchildren did something worthwhile. He loved us and we loved him.

# SOME SOUNDS
# AND SMELLS

Isn't it strange how certain sounds and smells linger in your memory? It's easy for me to close my eyes and hear the lonesome evening call of the whippoorwill. If you have ever heard this elusive bird, you'd recognize the call as it's very much like the spelling: whip-poor-will. This is definitely a sound of rural America and one I have not heard in a long time. In late May or early June, the female lays two eggs on the ground with scarcely more than a few leaves for a nest. The whippoorwill is a bird you rarely get to see. They are active in the evening and out of sight in the day.

There isn't much to the spring peeper, but when these tiny frogs join together, they can set off a mighty chorus. We are glad to hear the peeper, because they are a harbinger of spring.

It was in the woods near Uncle Walter's pond when I first heard the loud rhythmic hammering of the pileated woodpecker. It broke the silence of the woods like a machine gun. Never did I suspect a bird could cause such a noise. Hammering holes into the heart of the tree, they can leave a fair-sized pile of wood chips on the ground. I later learned they are in search of insects, usually carpenter ants, one of their main foods.

The rumble of a farm wagon traveling over a stony road has its own sound. This can be a rough ride if the road is very stony and you are sitting on the bed of the wagon. Sometimes I found it easier to get off and walk.

When a field of hay is mowed, something magical happens. It produces that wonderful smell of new-mown hay. Wonderful smell or not, Grandad would do something not many farmers would tolerate. He would take as many grandchildren who wanted to go along for a load of hay. Most of the hay was made on the Boorbaugh, so it was a nice long ride both ways. I suppose there were times when as many as 10 grandchildren rode that hay wagon. This was loose hay because Grandad didn't have a baler. Of course, those who were able were expected to pitch hay and help build the load so it wouldn't shift on the way to the barn. We were happy to hear Grandad say "I think that's enough." Up we would scramble to the top of the load and claim a spot for the ride back to the barn. I enjoyed lying on my back, looking up at the sky, smelling the hay, and listening to the wagon rumble down the hillside. That was one of life's simple pleasures I'll always remember.

The smoke house was the final step in the process of getting the hams, shoulders, and bacon ready to eat. Grandad preferred hickory or apple wood for producing smoke, and it had to be a slow, smoldering fire. A quick, hot fire would never do. Eventually, the meat turned a golden-rusty color. The old smoke house building had its own intense, appetizing odor. Today, liquid smoke is sold that you can rub on, but it can't top the smoke house method.

Kitchen smells on baking day could be downright tantalizing. Grandma's coal-fired stove produced some great pies, cookies, and especially homemade bread. Nothing was more satisfying to a hungry boy than a crust of homemade bread spread liberally with freshly churned butter. My grandmother and her daughter, Sarah Lucretia – my mother – were superior bakers. After many years of giving pie crusts the critical taste-test, I'm ready to proclaim Mom's pie crusts have never been equaled.

Working one summer in Blose Hollow cutting and sawing timber with Foster "Doc" Blose, I came to enjoy the smell of fresh sawdust. Like so many things in nature, it had its own clean, organic smell. There is a book recently published with the title "The Smell of Sawdust," by Richard J. Mouw. It's about evangelistic tent meetings and sawdust paths leading to the altar.

I'm reminded of the movie "Elmer Gantry" starring Burt Lancaster and Jean Simmons. It's about tent meetings and traveling evangelists. I saw the movie and thought it rather good.

Surely there are others beside myself who enjoy the smell of freshly turned earth. This can be following plowing or digging up root crops like potatoes, parsnips and turnips. I always enjoy harvesting root crops. The fruits of your labor remain hidden until harvest time. At the same time, you can enjoy the smell of newly turned earth.

# THE BOORBAUGH

Grandad owned 30 acres on top of a hill going west out of the valley. If I read the map correctly, it lies in Grant Township, Indiana County. He called this piece of land the "Boorbaugh." For Grandad, the word may have had a German meaning. You might describe it as a place where the spirits dwelled. He called one of them "Shinnerhaunis," a spirit to be feared if you misbehaved. We soon learned that Shinnerhaunis was imaginary and part of Grandad's sense of humor. Imaginary spirits or not, this is where Grandad grew most of his hay and grain crops.

One summer day I was hoeing corn with grandad on the Boorbaugh. The water we started out with in the earthen jug was getting warm. Grandad said "Let's see if there is any water in the upper spring." I didn't know an upper spring existed, but I was glad to stop hoeing and go in search of anything. He pointed to a tree and off we went. Sure enough, there was a trickle of water coming out of the earth below the tree. Using his hoe, he cleaned out a depression that soon filled with water. After the water cleared, Grandad took off his hat, got down on his knees, put his face to the water and drank his fill. When he got up, I did the same. Time has not erased the memory of that day at the upper spring. It remains the most refreshing drink of water I ever had, even if it might have failed today's health standards.

After our thirst was satisfied, Grandad said "Let's see if we can find the Wampler Graveyard." He took me on up the hill into the woods. Grandad soon found what he was looking for. There were several tombstones belonging to a Mrs. Wampler and her children. Some 60 years later, my cousins, Tom and Carolyn Blose and I made another trip to that same lonely hilltop in Grant Township. The tombstones were still there among a tangle of trees and brush. This time I took some pictures. The most legible tombstone reads "Margaret Ann, wife of E.C. Wampler. Died Oct. 6th 1864, Aged 28 yrs 10 mos and 7 ds." The other tombstones were not as easy to read. One is a son, Joseph C., another, a daughter, Agness Ann, and one marked Infant. All passed away in 1864. What caused all of them to die in the same year? What happened to the father, E.C. Wampler? This was during the Civil War, and that raises so many questions. I must write to the Indiana County Historical Society. They should be interested, especially because the graveyard is not one marked on the county map.

Also on the Boorbaugh was an excellent patch of huckleberries. This was the source of many wonderful pies and canned huckleberries for winter use. There seems to be some confusion between huckleberries and blueberries. The berries on the Boorbaugh were much sweeter but smaller than cultivated highbush blueberries. I believe them to be wild lowbush blueberries, and not whortleberries, as huckleberries are sometime called. Regardless of the name, they are delicious.

Several years ago, I climbed up and into the cab of a corn combine. In front of me were a number of levers and gauges having to do with operating the machine. Not only did it cut and shell the corn, it chewed up the stalks and spit them out the back end, and it registered the percentage of moisture in the corn and gave a running yield. I expect there was other information I have forgotten. When I left the combine, my mind went back to Grandad's corn field on the Boorbaugh before World War II. He didn't go into the field riding a machine. Grandad walked into the field with a single, small tool – a corn knife which was really a small machete. Each stalk was cut by hand and then shocked. Later, the ears would be hand-husked in the field or on the barn floor. I have in my desk a memento of those times. It is a husking peg you slip on your hand to help remove corn husks. I truly believe during those years we were witness to the most far-reaching agricultural revolution in all of human history; it began with Grandad walking into his corn field with a stalk-cutting knife or Grandad hoeing weeds in that same field, and ended with corn combines and weed sprayers made in factories that would soon be leaving farm factories ready to roll across the American farmland. What a technological revolution it has been.

# STONE FENCES
# AND NEW ROADS

When Henry Ford's Model T arrived, Grandad could expect more than one knock on the door in March, finding somebody standing there in muddy clothes and a forlorn look asking "Can you hitch up your team and pull me out of the mud?" Good dirt roads were fine for horses, but not Ford's new "Tin Lizzie." Mud in the spring and dust in the summer was more than the traveling public would tolerate.

In 1930, Gifford Pinchot was running for governor of Pennsylvania against John Hemphill, and he saw an opportunity in muddy roads. He campaigned on the promise to take Pennsylvania out of the mud. Pinchot won easily; the vote in Indiana County was 13,906 to 3,798.

Blose Hollow was in for one of Pinchot's new roads. This new blacktop hard-surfaced road needed a good foundation. Somebody remembered John Irwin's stone fences.

John Irwin had married Grandad's sister, Sadie. John and Sadie lived on a farm above the valley. They, along with their children, Josephine, Harry and John, wrestled a living out of one of the stoniest farms I have ever seen. The abundance of stone in the fields became fences. Over the years, John and his two sons built stone fences higher and wider than any I have seen, even in New England.

Some say John Irwin was a hard taskmaster, and his stone fences were the straw that broke the camel's back. His son John left home and worked in the West for many years before returning to the family home in Montgomery Township. A talented person, he never stayed long at one job. While in the West, John was in a serious vehicle accident, leaving him with a permanent limp. His brother, Harry, left home about the same time and never returned.

His disappearance was a tragic loss to his mother. She consulted fortunetellers and palmists for years with no success. Many years after her death, my Uncle Monroe discovered through a piece of misdirected mail that Harry Irwin was living in New York State. Uncle Monroe made a trip to New York and found his long-lost cousin working on a farm. Fate would have it that Harry never returned home, for he burned to death in a fire only a few months after he was located.

Had he returned, I wonder what Harry would have thought about the new hard-surfaced road in Blose Hollow. Stones from the fences that took years of his family's toil to build had become the foundation for that new road.

Machines had little to do with the building of the road. It was mostly manpower and horsepower. A large crew of men, stripped to the waist, broke tons and tons of rock with sledgehammers, reminding me of the hard labor that may have caused Harry to leave home. It also reminded me of the farmer who had some understanding of human nature when he said "If you want to keep your boy at home, don't bear too hard on the grindstone when he turns the crank."

I am grateful to my sister, Carol Ann Smith, for the following three stories. She was the youngest in our family and knew Grandad while I was in college. At that time, my parents were building a new home in Blose Hollow near Grandad's place. My folks lived with him until the house was finished, so Carol Ann may have known Grandad better than I did. You will notice she called him Grandpa, and not Grandad.

On many hot summer days, Grandpa and I would walk to Wilgus to Elmer Smith's store. I would be barefoot and getting tar on my feet because the heat from the sun made the tar on the road soft. I'm sure I must have complained about everything underfoot being so hot.

Grandpa and I would often stop at Ted Koozer's place – never went in. We would sit on the porch or under a tree while Grandpa and Ted exchanged conversation. After a while, we'd complete our walk to the store. We were never in a hurry. Just moseyed along.

I loved to enter the store. I can't explain the smell. All the smells ran together: those of cheese, the meats, everything on the shelves. I'm sure the smooth wooden counters soaked up the smells, too.

If Elmer wasn't to be seen, he would come out from behind curtains hanging in the doorway that separated the store from his living quarters. I always looked to see as much as I could of what was on the other side of the curtain. I could hear the radio playing. Elmer had a noticeable limp. One shoe was much higher than the other. Grandpa explained that one leg was shorter than the other, and that was why his shoes were a little different.

The big attraction for me was the candy counter. My treat was a BB bat. This was a sucker covered with little BB candies. I tried to make it last til we got home. Grandpa often bought a plug of tobacco.

We were tired from the heat and the walk. We would sit on the porch that stretched across the front of the house that was shaded by two big pine trees. We were both happy. Grandpa had his chew of tobacco. I had my BB bat.

# WALKING TO THE BARN

Who doesn't like to go outside when the stars are bright? I still remember Grandpa getting his lantern and lighting it. He would get a jacket if needed. Never had to get his hat because he always had it on. In fact, he slept in it. I know because I slept in the same room. There was a big room at the top of the stairs with two beds. One for Grandpa. One for me. As I remember, the beds were the only furniture. Maybe a small dresser and chair, too. When I got a little older, I moved next door. That room had a bed, a desk, a dresser and a mirror. I suppose I thought I needed the mirror. Getting a little older, you know. That was my bedroom until we moved to the stone house across the field.

Anyway, back to the stars and the lantern. When the lantern was lit I knew it was time to go to the barn to give Prince and Dick their bed snack and tell them goodnight. One day a truck came and took Dick away. Mom told me he was too old to work anymore. Not long afterwards, Nellie came to replace him. Grandpa always told me Prince was old enough to vote. In those days, that would be 21.

On our walk to the barn, we passed a big oak tree that was home to the swing Grandpa made for me. It was made from heavy, thick rope and had a board for my bottom. Not a plastic seat. A nice, big board — big enough to be comfortable and not pinch. The swing is gone but the big oak still stands. Grandpa always stopped to point out the Big Dipper and tell me that the bright star at the end of the handle was the North Star. I knew when it was about time to stop, and I'm sure if he had skipped it just one night, I would have been disappointed.

If you never have been in an old, quiet barn after dark and listened to the nicker of horses, you've missed a lot in my opinion. Grandpa always hung the lantern on a nail or wooden peg. It would sometimes create eerie shadows. He would give the horses their snack and they would nicker their thanks. We'd talk to them awhile and listen to the night barn sounds. And smell the barn smells. In the summer, that would be sweet hay.

It's been more than 50 years since my walks to the barn with Grandpa. He's gone now. The barn is gone. The place where it stood is grown up in grass and bushes. Some of the lumber is piled near by where the barn stood, but in my mind's eye, I can still see things as they were so many years ago.

# WALNUTS
# IN THE CEMETARY

Grandpa often told this story.

Just inside the fence surrounding an old cemetery stood a walnut tree. one evening two boys came and gathered a bucketful of walnuts. They sat down by the tree, out of sight, and began dividing the nuts: "One for you, one for me, one for you, one for me." Before long it became dark and several walnuts dropped and rolled through the fence.

Another boy came riding along the road on his bicycle. As he passed, he thought he heard voices from inside the cemetery and slowed down to investigate. Sure enough, he heard, "One for you, one for me, one for you, one for me."

He knew just what was going on. He jumped back on his bike and rode off. Just around the curve he met an old man hobbling along with a cane. "Come quick," said the boy, "You won't believe what I heard! The Devil and the Lord are in the cemetery dividing up the dead."

The old man said, "I'm crippled and can't walk very far." When the boy insisted, the man hobbled on to the cemetery. Standing by the cemetery fence they heard, "One for you, one for me, one for you, one for me..."

The old man whispered, "Boy, you've been telling the truth. Let's see if we can see the Lord." Shaking with fear they peered through the fence but couldn't see a thing.

At last they heard, "One for you, one for me. That's all. Now let's get those outside the fence."

They say the old man made it back to town a full five minutes ahead of the boy on the bike.

# END OF AN ERA

Richard Ifft, former Indiana County agricultural agent with the Penn State Cooperative Extension Service, once said to me "Bill, we both know a crow flying over Montgomery Township would have to carry its lunch to keep from starving." Certainly an exaggeration, but still there was a kernel of truth in his statement.

The land in Blose Hollow is not suited to the big farm machinery being manufactured today. The fields and slopes are too small and steep to justify investing in farm equipment really designed for the Midwest.

When I saw Grandad hang up his grain cradle for the last time, little did I realize I was witness to the end of an era. A centuries-old system of agriculture and the day of the self-sufficient family farm were coming to an end. When Grandad cradled grain, all he had to supply was skill and human endurance. To buy one of the new grain binders would take considerable cash, and that he didn't have.

Most of the power needed on Grandad's farm came from the family and a team of draft horses. Most of the essentials needed they produced themselves. They had no automobile or tractor and no need for gasoline. Fuel for the horses was oats and hay, and that was grown at home.

In my mind's eye I can still plainly see some of Grandad's farm implements. One was a hand hoe he used in the corn field. Repeated sharpenings over the years and the stony ground had reduced the size of that hoe to one-fourth its original size. People don't hoe corn anymore. Weeds are eliminated with chemicals. Like Grandad's grain cradle, the hoe, flail, wooden rake and so many other things have become museum pieces.

For a number of years, Indiana County has been known as the "Christmas Tree Capitol of the World." A group of local nurserymen, along with the Penn State extension agent, made a concerted effort to promote the growing of quality Christmas trees. Because of their work and leadership, Indiana County became the center of the Christmas tree industry. During high school, my brothers and I hired out to plant Christmas trees on Saturday for one dollar an hour. That was great money in those days.

The topography of Blose Hollow is well suited for Christmas trees. My two brothers bought a farm near to Uncle Walter's old homestead and subsequently sold it to Musser Forests. Today, the entire farm is trees. Perhaps, in the future, Christmas trees will occupy more land in the valley. In the meantime, those living there are either retired or have jobs somewhere else.

At the beginning of this family story, I said the people who settled Blose Hollow were bound to a way of life dictating they "Use it up, wear it out, make it do or do without." Today, that statement has little meaning.

We live in a quick-fix, disposable, government-owes-me-a-living society. If it doesn't work, throw it away. Unfortunately, this applies to people as well as things. If somebody wrongs us, we call a lawyer or write our congressman.

Our wants become our needs. Nobody plays on this human weakness more than politicians. Many of them bribe us with promises of cradle-to-the-grave protection in exchange for our vote. Something all too rare is a statesman-like challenge for us to sacrifice for the good of our country.

Most of the early pioneers who settled this great land were young and they were poor. Their possessions were few but they were courageous, self-reliant and possessed an indomitable spirit. We desperately need their spirit.

# ABOUT THE AUTHOR

Bill King is a native of Indiana County, Pennsylvania, and a graduate of Clymer High School. He served in the U.S. Navy during World War II.

Bill is a graduate of Penn State University where he received both a bachelor's and master's degree in animal science. While doing graduate work he was an instructor in animal science. In 1955 he went to Armstrong County, PA as an agricultural agent with the Penn State University Extension Service. Upon retirement in 1985, he was County Extension Director and Senior Extension Agent. After retiring, Bill became a self-taught photographer. Among his many photographic endeavors is a book titled "Armstrong County, A Place for all Seasons."